MY DEN MOTHER IS

MY DEN DAD IS

MY DEN CHIEF IS

I AM CUB SCOUT

1959 REVISION

WOLF CUB SCOUT BOOK

Copyright 1954 by the

BOY SCOUTS

NEW BRUNSWICK

No. 3230—45 Cents

O F A M E R I C A

NEW JERSEY

PRINTED IN U.S.A.

650M1059

CONTENTS

ELECTIVES

ON YOUR CUB SCOUT UNIFORM YOU CAN WEAR

1. Your community strip.

2. Your Pack numeral.

3. Your Bobcat or Wolf badge when you earn it.

4. Arrow Points when you earn them.

5. Your Den numeral.

You'll take pride in your appearance in your new Cub Scout uniform, because when you wear it people will know you are a Cub Scout growing straight and strong through Cub Scouting. Remember — there is only one official uniform—there are no substitutes.

HOW TO JOIN

Are you eight years old? If you are, you may join the Cub Scouts.

First you become a Bobcat. This means you are a new Cub Scout.

Then you wear the Bobcat badge. That is a button with a Bobcat head on it. See it in the picture below. Wear it centered on the left shirt pocket of your uniform until you earn your Wolf badge. You may also wear it on your everyday clothes.

You cannot get the Bobcat badge just by asking for it. Cub Scout badges must be earned.

Here are the five things you do to earn your Bobcat badge:

1. Learn and give the Cub Scout Promise.

2. Say the Law of the Pack. Tell what it means.

3. Tell what Webelos means.

4. Show the Cub Scout sign and handshake. Tell what they mean.

5. Give the Cub Scout Motto and salute. Tell what they mean.

These five things are explained on pages 4 to 11. Ask your dad or mother to read those pages with you. Then ask them to read pages 153 to 157 with you. There you will learn about your Den and your Pack.

PROMISE

When you promise to do something, you mean you will do it. Even if it is hard, a Cub Scout keeps his promise. He wants people to believe him.

DO MY BEST

When you say, "I will DO MY BEST," you mean, "I will try as hard as I can." One boy's best can be better than another boy's best. Cub Scout leaders do not expect you to be perfect. They want you to do your best.

When you do your DUTY, you do your share. You do what you ought to do.

DUTY TO GOD

Your duty to GOD is done with God's help. It means you practice your religion at home, in the church or synagogue, in everything you do.

DUTY TO COUNTRY

Your duty to your COUNTRY means to be a good American. Our country's laws take care of the rights that God gives to everybody in the world.

BE SQUARE

This means be fair to everybody. Sometimes this is not easy. But a Cub Scout will always try to be square. He wants everybody to be fair to him, so he is fair to everybody.

OBEY THE LAW OF THE PACK

The Law of the Pack has four ideas for a Cub Scout to use everyday. When you use these ideas, you OBEY the Law of the Pack. See the Law of the Pack. Read about it on page 7.

CUB SCOUT PROMISE

I ~~Joe~~ *Gregory* PROMISE

TO DO MY BEST

TO DO MY DUTY

TO GOD AND
MY COUNTRY,

TO BE SQUARE,
AND

TO OBEY THE LAW
OF THE PACK

Talk with your parents about the Cub Scout Promise and the Law of the Pack. Ask your Den Mother to talk with your Den about the Promise and the Law.

LAW OF THE PACK

THE CUB SCOUT *FOLLOWS* AKELA

THE CUB SCOUT *HELPS* THE PACK GO

THE PACK *HELPS* THE CUB SCOUT GROW

THE CUB SCOUT *GIVES* GOOD WILL

6

FOLLOWS AKELA

Who is AKELA? (Say Ah-kay-la)

AKELA is a Cub Scout name for a good leader. A leader is someone you follow. Some of the people you may call AKELA are your father or mother, your teacher, your Den Chief, your Den Mother or Cubmaster, or anybody who is a good leader.

Most good leaders first learned to follow. That's why the first part of the Law of the Pack asks you to learn to follow. Follow good leaders. Follow AKELA.

HELPS THE PACK GO

When you become a Cub Scout, you are no longer just a boy. Now you are a member of a Den and a Pack. You can't think only of yourself, but you must think also of your fellow Cub Scouts.

Help the Pack GO by coming to all meetings, by following the leaders, and by making your Pack in every way better because you are in it.

HELPS THE CUB SCOUT GROW

You will have a lot of fun when you join the Pack. You will learn things from other people, and you will learn to do things with them. That's real fun! You help the Pack GO, and the Pack helps you GROW.

GIVES GOOD WILL

You will find that if you smile at your friends, they will smile back at you. If you are friendly to them, they will be friendly to you.

Look for things to do for other people. They need not be big things, but just little things that help.

Smile and help—these are two fine Cub Scout words.

CUB SCOUT CODE

BUC
TUOCS
EDOC

A code is a set of secret words. When you are a Cub Scout, you can write to another Cub Scout with the Cub Scout code.

GNITIRW SDRAWKCAB

That's right — you guessed it! It's writing backwards.

CUB SCOUT SIGN

Make the sign with your right hand held high, straight up above your shoulder. This is the sign of the Cub Scout all over the world. The two top fingers stand for the two parts of the Promise.

THE HANDSHAKE

When you shake hands with another Cub Scout, hold out your right hand just as you usually do to shake hands. Put your first two fingers along the inside of the other boy's wrist. This means that he, too, is square and obeys the Law of the Pack.

THE SALUTE

A salute is a way to say hello to your leaders. It is a polite way to show that you like them. We salute the Flag because it stands for how we live in America.

Salute with your right hand. Hold your fingers as you do for the Cub Scout sign. Keep the two straight fingers close together. Then touch the tips of those fingers to your cap.

THE LIVING CIRCLE

You do the living circle with the other Cub Scouts of your Den. Hold out your left hand with the palm down and the thumb out. Hold the thumb of the boy on your left. Hold up your right hand in the Cub Scout sign.

The living circle means that all Cub Scouts are friends.

WEBELOS

Webelos sounds like an Indian name, doesn't it? (Say Wee-buh-lows.) It is the name of the Indian tribe where Akela is chief. Webelos has a secret meaning.

W   B   L   S

are the first letters of: Wolf, Bear, Lion, Scout.
When you are eight, you earn the Wolf badge.
When you are nine, you earn the Bear badge.
When you are ten, you earn the Lion badge.
When you are ten and a half, you earn the Webelos badge.

Here is a picture of the Webelos badge.

See the Indian sign for the sun above the arrow. That is why the badge is called the arrow of light. It lights the trail you follow to become a Boy Scout. The Webelos badge means you are ready to be a Boy Scout when you are eleven years old.

THE MOTTO

"DO YOUR BEST" is the Cub Scout Motto. It means when you play a game, do your best. When you study in school, do your best. When you help at home, do your best. Always do your best.

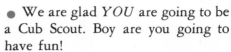

HELLO!

● We are glad *YOU* are going to be a Cub Scout. Boy are you going to have fun!

● You like to play games don't you? Well, you came to the right place. Cub Scouts play lots of games.

● Making things is OK with you, too. With the Cub Scouts you can make boats, airplanes, Indian suits, and other things you like.

● It's fun to make believe. Cub Scouts in their meetings make believe they are cowboys, Indians, space cadets, firemen, policemen, knights, almost any kind of hero.

● Do you know what a cookout is? It is a meal cooked outside—in the backyard or a park—by Cub Scouts and their fathers.

● Sometimes Cub Scout families go on a picnic. So we say again, we are glad *YOU* are going to be a Cub Scout. Boy, are you going to have fun!

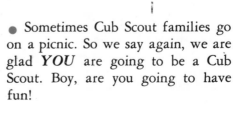

THE WOLF

L et's make believe you lived 200 years ago. Suppose your father was an Indian chief and your mother was an Indian woman. You would have to learn the secrets of the Great Forest by going into it yourself.

You would have to follow the tracks of the Wolf to learn the way he lives.

On the trail you would see and learn many things.

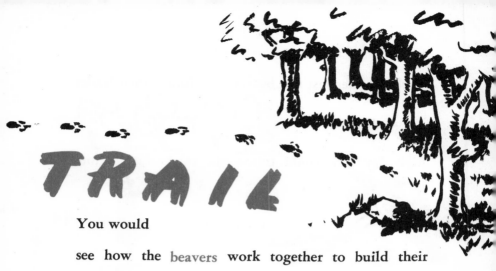

TRAIL

You would

see how the beavers work together to build their

mighty dam.

You would watch the geese in flight, following

their leader.

By a stream you would stop to watch Indians build

a big

war

canoe.

They would

work together just like beavers and follow their leader
just as the geese do.

Each day you would follow the tracks farther into

the forest. Each

day you could jump across a wider stream or climb a

taller tree. You would be

getting   stronger

and   stronger.

You would learn  more and more

about the rocks, trees, birds, and animals. Your

adventure would not always be in the woods. One

day it might   be at the side of the men who make

arrows. They would teach you to make arrows. Another

day you  might learn to

weave a  blanket or build a tepee.

Each night you would tell the story of your adventure to your father and mother. They would praise you. They would tell you how to be ready for a bigger adventure tomorrow.

"But I'm not an Indian boy!" you say. Well, that's true, but your teacher helps you learn things you can't find out for yourself.

Your mother can help you do many useful things about the house.

Your father can help you make things with tools.

He can play ball or go fishing with you.

When you do these things, you follow the Wolf
trail.

There are other people who will help you. Your
Cubmaster will show you the way. Your Den Mother
will help you make things like the arrow makers made.

Your Den Chief will help you to learn to jump
like the deer,   run like
the fox,   and build like
the beaver.

Follow the Wolf Trail through this book. You will
get the fun and thrills the Indian boy had when he
went into the Great Forest.

HOW TO FOLLOW THE WOLF TRAIL

1. The Wolf Trail is divided into twelve parts. Each part is called an achievement.

2. Do you know what an achievement is? It is something you do or make. You will find the twelve achievements on pages 18 to 47.

3. Your Den Mother and your Den Chief may help you start an achievement. But your dad and mother will help you most.

4. One of your parents has to watch you do each achievement. He will want you to "DO YOUR BEST."

5. When you finish an achievement, turn to it in this book. Ask the parent who watched you do the achievement to sign for it.

Charlene Hunter

MOTHER OR DAD SIGN HERE

6. Then take your Wolf book to your Den meeting. Show your Den Mother where your dad or mother signed for your new achievement.

7. When you do all twelve Wolf achievements, you become a Wolf Cub Scout, and you get the Wolf Cub Scout badge from your dad or mother at the Pack meeting.

FEATS OF SKILL

ACHIEVEMENT 1

You like to have fun and grow strong. That is why you will like Feats of Skill. They are clever tricks you do with your body.

The rolls will help you fall without getting hurt. The climbs will make your arms and legs strong. Learning to walk the 2″ x 4″ board will strengthen your eyes and help keep you from falling.

Start each feat slowly. Try to do better each time.

Complete any three of the following:

1. Do a front roll, back roll, and falling forward roll.

2. Play catch with someone twenty feet away. Play until you can throw and catch well.

3. Climb at least twelve feet up a tree.

4. Swim thirty feet in shallow water. Also by holding a "kick board" or other floating support, move thirty feet through the water by kicking only. Do both of these with a grown-up who swims well.

5. Practice walking on a line forward, sideways and reverse directions until you can walk a 2″ x 4″ board twelve feet each way.

Charlene Hunter

MOTHER OR DAD SIGN HERE

Charlene Hunter, 64

FRONT ROLL

BEND

Tuck head in to one side and then over in a ball

BACK ROLL

CURL BACKWARD   PUSH   AND ROLL

FALLING FORWARD ROLL

DIVE   TUCK YOUR HEAD   ROLL OVER AND UP

NOTE TO PARENTS. Where a licensed physician certifies that the Cub Scout's physical condition for an indeterminable time doesn't permit him to do three of the requirements in this achievement, the Cubmaster and the Pack Committee may authorize substitutions of any three of the Arrow Point electives.

TREE CLIMBING

You can go up small tree trunks by pulling yourself up a little at a time and by getting a strong foot hold.

Unless you can leap like a squirrel, don't get out on the end of a limb.

Test the branches before putting your full weight on them. Never trust dead branches!

"KICK BOARD SWIM"

Grasp kick board firmly. Shove off bottom with feet as you straighten out in water with legs outstretched, move feet slowly up and down, past each other. Keep practicing this kick until you get your proper rhythm. Kick your legs and paddle with your hands a little if you have to. Speed it up then until you can kick evenly and rapidly.

FLAG

When you salute your flag, you salute a lot of other things too. You salute your family, your home, your friends, and your Cub Scout Den. You salute the farms, the rivers, the mountains, the plains. You salute all these things when you salute your flag, because they are America!

1. Give the Pledge of Allegiance to the flag of the United States of America.

2. Conduct a flag ceremony in your Den.
   The Pledge of Allegiance and ceremony are explained on pages 22 and 23.

MOTHER OR DAD SIGN HERE

Charlene Hunter ✓ 64
Charlene Hunter

21

PLEDGE
OF ALLEGIANCE

"I pledge allegiance to the flag of the United States of America and to the Republic for which it stands, one Nation under God, indivisible, with liberty and justice for all."

This Pledge is a promise you are giving. *Allegiance* means being true to our country. *Republic* means the way our people rule themselves. The *nation* is our country. *Indivisible* means our country can not be broken into more than one country. *Liberty* for all means letting everybody in America be free. *Justice* for all means being fair to everybody.

Ask your parents to tell you what they think about this Pledge of Allegiance.

A flag ceremony is a special way we salute the flag. Here are a few Den flag ceremonies. You can make up others.

1. The Den stands in a straight line and faces the flag. All the boys give the Cub Scout salute and say the Pledge of Allegiance to the flag.

2. The Den stands in a hollow square. A Cub Scout brings the flag into the square. The other boys salute and say the Cub Scout Promise.

3. The Den stands in a circle around the flag. Then the boys salute the flag and say the Pledge of Allegiance.

KEEPING WELL

ACHIEVEMENT 3

To have fun and do all the things that Cub Scouts like to do, you must be active and feel *good*.

In passing this achievement you will follow the simple health rules and keep well and strong.

You will also learn how to take care of a small cut on your finger.

1. Understand and follow the rules for keeping clean.

2. Show what to do for a small cut on your hand.

3. Have a health checkup by a doctor (optional).

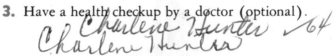

Charlene Hunter /64

MOTHER OR DAD SIGN HERE

RULES FOR KEEPING WELL

TEETH—Brush them every morning and night. Brush them after each meal or rinse your mouth. See your dentist twice a year.

HANDS AND NAILS—Wash before eating or going to bed, and always after going to toilet. Keep nails clean, trimmed.

KEEP CLEAN

Take a bath regularly. When you wash, use soap.

BODY — INSIDE

Water is good for you—Drink lots.

LET IT BLEED

TAKE CARE OF CUTS

Wash them gently with soap and water. Cover with a clean dressing. Hold in place with a bandage or adhesive tape.

HEALTH CHECK-UP

Your dad's car needs a checkup every few months. You, too, need a checkup with a doctor every year. He can catch little troubles before they become big troubles.

NOTE TO PARENTS!

While a doctor's examination is not required for this achievement, it is strongly recommended. Certainly a growing boy should have a health checkup every year. Discover and stop trouble, if there is any, before it becomes serious!

HELPS IN THE HOME

ACHIEVEMENT 4

You are no longer just a "little boy" when you are eight years old. You are able to do more than you did when you were six or seven.

Why don't you ask your mother and dad how you can help around home? Maybe you can tell them some things you'd like to do.

"The Cub Scout gives good will." This achievement gives you a chance to live up to the Cub Scout Promise and the Law of the Pack. You'll find out how much fun it is helping others.

Can you cut the grass, rake leaves, carry in wood for the fireplace, wash dishes, or sweep the sidewalk? The important thing is, do it as often as it needs doing.

1. Talk with mother and dad about helping around home. Pick the home jobs that you will do. Keeping your own things in order would be one. Also, agree on time for this work. Make a chart to keep a record of what you do. (A sample chart is at the bottom of this page.)

2. Do your best to live up to the Cub Scout Promise and the Law of the Pack.

MOTHER OR
DAD SIGN HERE

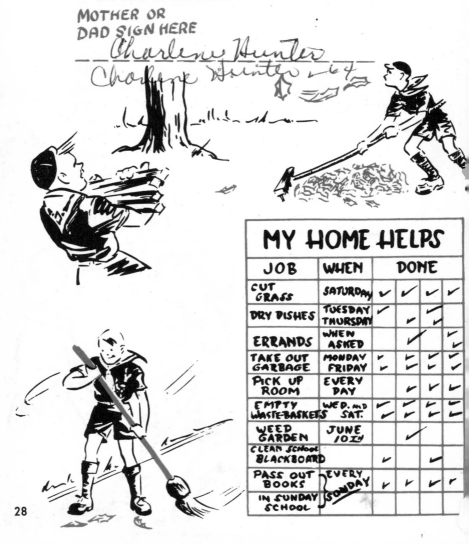

MY HOME HELPS

JOB	WHEN	DONE			
CUT GRASS	SATURDAY	✓	✓	✓	✓
DRY DISHES	TUESDAY THURSDAY	✓		✓	✓
ERRANDS	WHEN ASKED			✓	✓
TAKE OUT GARBAGE	MONDAY FRIDAY	✓ ✓	✓	✓	✓ ✓
PICK UP ROOM	EVERY DAY		✓	✓	✓
EMPTY WASTE-BASKETS	WED. AND SAT.	✓ ✓	✓	✓ ✓	✓ ✓
WEED GARDEN	JUNE 10 14		✓		
CLEAN SCHOOL BLACKBOARD		✓		✓	
PASS OUT BOOKS IN SUNDAY SCHOOL	EVERY SUNDAY	✓	✓	✓	✓

WHITTLING

ACHIEVEMENT 5

Ask your dad if he had a jackknife when he was your age. He can show you how to keep your knife clean and shiny and sharp.

Ask him what he made with his jackknife. Maybe he'll help you make something, too.

1. Show that you know how to take care of and use a jackknife.

2. Make something with it.

MOTHER OR DAD

SIGN HERE _ _ _ _ *Charlene Hunter*

PUSH
AWAY
FROM
YOU

JACKKNIFE CARE

Close blade with palm of hand. Always cut away from you. Never drive your knife into a stick by hammering on it.

OIL

HOW TO CLEAN

OIL ON RAG

SHARP EDGE

HOW TO KEEP A KNIFE SHARP

Rub one side of blade back and forth slowly over a sharpening stone. Hold the back edge of the blade just a little off the stone. Turn the blade over and do the same on the other side.

NECKERCHIEF SLIDES

FLAT WOOD CUT-OUTS AND ROPE

BRANCH SECTION WITH PITHY STEM

TWIG AND ROPE

COLLECTIONS

Some time take all the things out of your pockets. Put them on a table in front of you. It's quite a collection, isn't it?

A boy we knew had some green glass, a fishhook, a top, a knife, four buttons, two marbles, and a frog, all in one pocket. When his mother patched his pants, she put her hand in this pocket. You should have heard her squeal when she touched the frog.

In Cub Scouting you'll learn how to gather things for a collection. You will learn to keep and show these things neatly. Pick something you will have fun collecting.

Your dad collected things when he was a boy, too. Ask him to give you some ideas.

1. Make a collection of anything you wish. Talk to dad and mother and decide how many things will make a good collection.

2. Mark the name beside each thing in your collection.

Charlene Hunter 64

Charlene Hunter ____

MOTHER OR DAD SIGN HERE

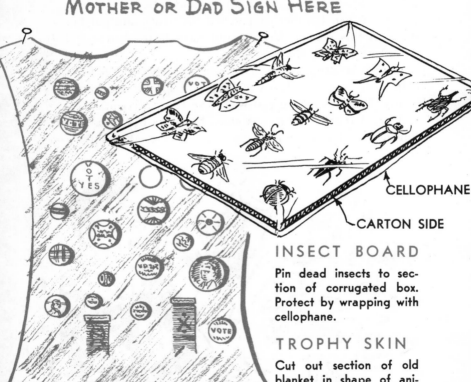

CELLOPHANE

CARTON SIDE

INSECT BOARD

Pin dead insects to section of corrugated box. Protect by wrapping with cellophane.

TROPHY SKIN

Cut out section of old blanket in shape of animal skin. Attach buttons, medals, awards, pins, souvenirs, etc. Hang on wall in your room.

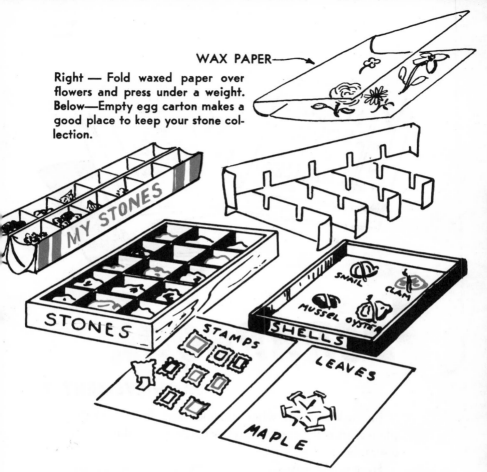

Right — Fold waxed paper over flowers and press under a weight. Below—Empty egg carton makes a good place to keep your stone collection.

WAX PAPER

MY STONES

STONES

SHELLS

SNAIL   CLAM

MUSSEL   OYSTER

STAMPS

LEAVES

MAPLE

HOW TO KEEP AND SHOW YOUR COLLECTIONS

STONES
  Put them in a tray with cardboard fences.
SHELLS
  Wire them on a cardboard in a tray.
STAMPS
  Use sticky paper hinges to fasten them in a book.
TREE LEAVES
  Put them in a book with sticky tape. Write the name beside each leaf.

SCRAPBOOK

ACHIEVEMENT 7

Just ask yourself what you like best. Is it baseball, airplanes, animals, cars, trains? Whatever you like best, make a scrapbook of it.

Here is one way.

Get twenty-five sheets of paper and two pieces of cardboard. Fasten them together with the cardboard for covers. Use heavy string, rings, or wire. See the pictures at the top of the page. If you like baseball, cut out baseball pictures from magazines and newspapers. Write in about your own games. Keep a record of your scores. If you like airplanes cut out and paste in pictures of planes and airports. You can also write about different planes you have seen and read about.

Start saving souvenirs and snapshots of your Cub Scout activities now in preparation for the Lion Achievement 7, Log Book.

1. Make a scrapbook with at least twenty-five pages.
2. Put in your own drawings, stories, snapshots, and pictures from magazines and newspapers.

Charlene Hunter

MOTHER OR DAD SIGN HERE

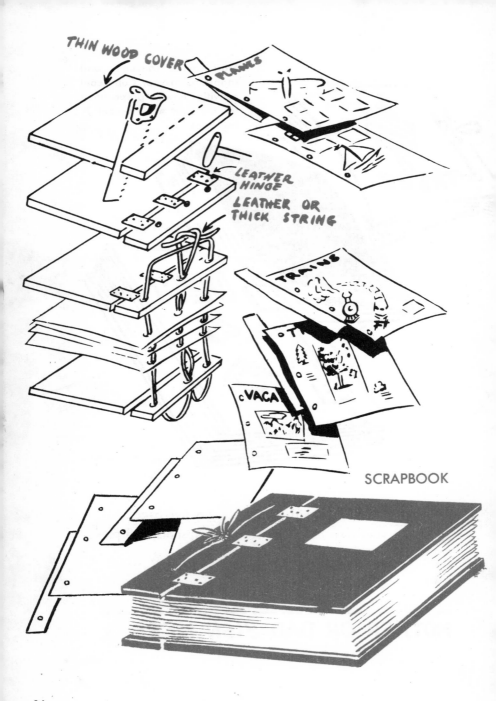

THIN WOOD COVER

PLANES

LEATHER HINGE

LEATHER OR THICK STRING

TRAINS

VACA

SCRAPBOOK

TYING THINGS

ACHIEVEMENT 8

A boy your age wants to take care of himself. You want to tie your own necktie without your mother's help. You want to tie your own shoelaces so they will stay. There is a special knot to use, you know. If the bows are up and down, it's a poor knot. If the bows sit across your shoe, then you've tied a good bow knot.

Other things in this achievement will help you to help yourself and other folks. You will learn to tie a package neatly. Then you can help mother wrap and tie up gifts.

1. Wrap and tie a package so that it is neat and tight.

2. Tie your shoestrings with a square knot or a shoe knot.

3. Tie your necktie. *Charlene Hunter*

4. Tie two pieces of cord together with an overhand knot.

Charlene Hunter

MOTHER OR DAD SIGN HERE

TIE YOUR TIE RIGHT

WRAPPING A PACKAGE

Make a neat pile of things on the center of the paper. Fold over the long sides of the paper, then fold in the ends tightly. Tie the string with a square knot.

OVERHAND KNOT

Tie two cords together with an overhand knot.

TIE YOUR SHOELACES

Tie your shoelaces in a good bow knot.

SAFETY

Hundreds of people are killed every year by falling down stairs. Do you know why? It's because many boys leave their things on the stairs. Even some grown-ups leave things on the stairs. You can help keep your family from being hurt. Just see that nothing is ever left on the stairs in your home. Don't do this for only a few days. Keep at it all the time.

1. Inspect your home with mother or dad and help them remove possible causes of accidents.

2. Practice home safety by keeping storerooms, closets, attic, or basement clear of fire and accident hazards.

3. Practice rules of fire safety.

Charlene Hunter

MOTHER OR DAD SIGN HERE

CELLAR

NO RAILING ON STAIRS. UP-TURNED RAKE ON FLOOR. BE SURE THERE'S A LIGHT!

KITCHEN

KEEP KNIVES IN SAFE KNIFE-HOLDER, NOT LOOSE IN DRAWER. BE CAREFUL AROUND STOVE.

RULES FOR FIRE SAFETY

1. DON'T PLAY WITH MATCHES.

2. KEEP GASOLINE AND OTHER DANGEROUS THINGS AWAY FROM FIRES OR STRONG HEAT.

3. KEEP MATCHES WHERE SMALL CHILDREN CANNOT REACH THEM.

4. DESTROY ALL WASTE MATERIALS — ESPE-CIALLY GREASE OR OILY RAGS.

5. BE SURE ALL ELECTRIC WIRING, SWITCHES, FUSES, AND FIXTURES ARE O.K.

6. KNOW WHERE THE NEAREST FIRE ESCAPES ARE IN ALL BUILDINGS YOU ENTER.

7. BE SURE YOUR OUTDOOR FIRE IS COM-PLETELY OUT BEFORE YOU LEAVE IT.

ATTIC

LOOSE PAPERS
CATCH FIRE
EASILY

EXIT

KNOW
WHERE
EXITS ARE

OLD, FRAYED
WIRE IS
DANGEROUS

KEEP MATCHES
IN SAFE PLACE

KEEP GASO-
LINE AND OIL
AWAY FROM
FIRE

PUT ALL
FIRES OUT

GASOL

41

HOME GAMES

ACHIEVEMENT 10

Home is a place where you like to be when there is something interesting to do.

You and your dad can make a homemade game. Then your family can play it together. It's better than buying a game.

Or maybe you would rather get your family to help you plan an afternoon walk. No matter what season of the year it is, there is something to see. You can play a game while you're out on the walk. Who will see the first bird or the first animal? Who will find the first bird or animal track?

1. Make a homemade indoor game and play it with your family.

OR

2. Plan and go on a family walk or picnic.

Charlene Hunter

MOTHER OR DAD
SIGN HERE   *Charlene Hunter*

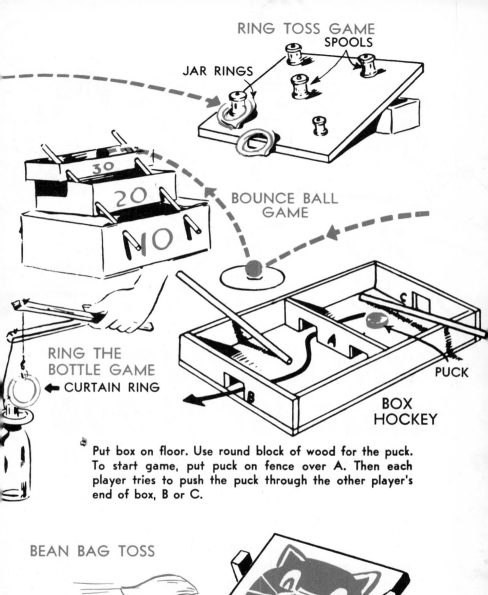

RING TOSS GAME

SPOOLS

JAR RINGS

BOUNCE BALL
GAME

30

20

NO

RING THE
BOTTLE GAME
← CURTAIN RING

C

PUCK

B

BOX
HOCKEY

Put box on floor. Use round block of wood for the puck.
To start game, put puck on fence over A. Then each
player tries to push the puck through the other player's
end of box, B or C.

BEAN BAG TOSS

KNOW YOUR NEIGHBORHOOD
ACHIEVEMENT 11

To help other people find places, you should know where things are in your neighborhood. The neighborhood is the part of the city, or small town, or open country where you live.

If you see a fire, do you know where to find the fire station or a fire alarm box? If you see an accident, do you know where to find a policeman or a sheriff? Find out all you can about your neighborhood. Then you can tell people how to find places.

If some of the persons and things in number one below cannot be found in your town, try to discover the nearest place where they can be found.

1. Show that you know where to find and how to reach the following:
   Nearest fire station or fire alarm box; nearest constable, sheriff, policeman, or police station; public telephone; bus or trolley stops; doctor; railroad station; gas stations; nearby highways or main streets; hospital; post office.

2. Show that you can give clear directions to auto drivers or people on the street to the above spots from anywhere near your home.

MOTHER OR DAD SIGN HERE   *Charlene Hunter*

Charlene Hunter

READING

ACHIEVEMENT 12

There are a lot of things you wish you might do. Maybe you wish to hunt lions. Maybe you wish to be Robin Hood in Sherwood Forest. Maybe you wish to be an airplane pilot or ball player.

It would be wonderful if all of your wishes came true. You can come close to doing these things by reading about them. A good book about lion hunting can almost take you into the jungle. Tell your teacher or librarian some of the things you'd like to do. She can tell you some fine books to read about those things. Also see the book list in the back.

1. Ask your parents, teacher, or librarian to help you make up a list of books. Read two of the books.

2. Learn how to take care of books and how to open a new book.

3. Tell a story to your Den.

MOTHER or DAD
SIGN HERE ➤ _Charlene Hunter_
Charlene Hunter 64

You Are Now A

WOLF CUB SCOUT

How You Can Earn

ARROW POINTS

When you finish the twelve Wolf achievements you get your Wolf badge.

THEN

Comes more fun. . . . You can earn Arrow Points to wear under your new badge.

You will need ten credits to earn your Gold Arrow Point.

Ten more credits will qualify you for a Silver Arrow Point.

A credit is given each time you do one of the things listed under an "elective."

There are twenty-three electives for you to choose from.

You'll find out about them on pages 54 to 143. Many of them you and dad can work on together, or maybe you and mother, or perhaps someone else in the family can help you. Other people who will help you are your Den Mother, Den Chief, Den Dad, and teacher. Ask questions of anyone who can help you. To show you how elective credits add up, let's look below:

You will get one credit every time you finish one item listed in the elective you choose.

You may like boats so well you want to make a whole fleet of them. So each time you finish a boat you get a credit toward your Arrow Point.

Of course, dad and mom will insist that you make each boat better than the last one you made, even though it's the same model.

In other words — you can earn an Arrow Point by getting ten credits in as many as ten different electives. OR — by getting ten credits in as few as one elective. You see, you can skip around and do the electives that you like. Fun, isn't it?

Remember dad or mother had to watch you do the achievements and sign for them. Well, they watch you do things for electives, too.

Suppose dad watches you make and fly a kite for the Kites elective. At the bottom of page 76 he writes "1" in the credit circle. Beside it, he puts his initial and the date, like this:

Each time you do one of the items suggested under an elective, you will receive an Arrow Point credit. In the box score on the next page write in the name of the elective and number of item completed for each credit.

For example, when you complete the Kites elective item listed above, "Make and fly a kite," fill in your box score as follows:

ELECTIVE   ITEM

Kites   1

When you have ten credits, you will receive your Gold Arrow Point. Wear it under your Wolf badge. For each additional ten credits, you will receive a Silver Arrow Point. There is no limit to the number of Silver Arrow Points you may earn. Keep your box score below.

ELECTIVE	ITEM	ELECTIVE	ITEM

GOLD ARROW POINT RECD.

DATE

SILVER ARROW POINT RECD.

DATE

Take this book to Den meeting. Show your Den Mother that another box score is filled. Then at the Pack meeting you will be given the Arrow Point by your parents.

Look again at the electives on pages 54 to 143. Those pages are packed with interesting things for you to do. That's all electives are—interesting things to do. Pick the thing you like best, and start having fun.

HOW THE ELECTIVE

You can earn an Arrow Point by getting ten credits in as many as ten different electives.

ONE CREDIT

ONE CREDIT

ELECTIVE 6

MAKE A BOAT

ONE CREDIT

ELECTIVE 1

A SECRET CODE AND INVISIBLE WRITING

ONE CREDIT

ONE CREDIT

ONE CREDIT

ELECTIVE 13

DRAW A CARTOON, SCENE, DECORATE YOUR ROOM

ONE CREDIT

ELECTIVE 19

COOK YOUR OWN BREAKFAST

ONE CREDIT

ONE CREDIT

ELECTIVE 10

TABLE DECORATIONS

ONE CREDIT

ELECTIVE 3

MAKE SOMETHING USEFUL

CREDITS ADD UP

OR—by getting ten credits in as few as one elective.

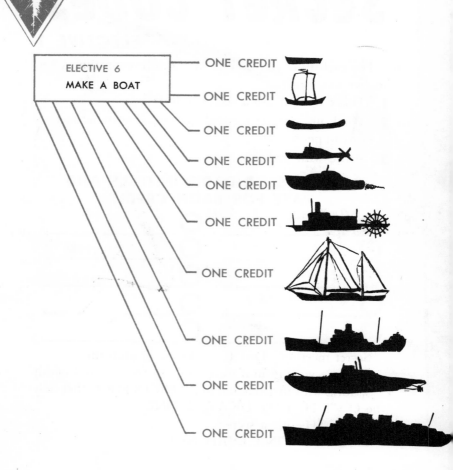

ELECTIVE 6
MAKE A BOAT

ONE CREDIT

ONE CREDIT

ONE CREDIT

ONE CREDIT

ONE CREDIT

ONE CREDIT

ONE CREDIT

ONE CREDIT

ONE CREDIT

ONE CREDIT

SECRET CODES

ELECTIVE 1

For each time you do one of the following things you receive *one credit*.

1. Think up and use a secret code.
2. Think up a secret method of communication, such as tin can phones, etc.
3. Write with invisible ink.

MOTHER'S OR DAD'S INITIALS AND DATE FOR EACH CREDIT

① BH 17 JAN 62 ◯ _____
② BH 17 JAN 62 ◯ _____
③ BH 17 JAN 62 ◯ _____
◯ _____ ◯ _____
◯ _____ ◯ _____

Secret meeting—Den 1 . . . Come in uniform . . .

Imagine writing in a secret code to your trusted buddy —writing with invisible ink in a TERCES EDOC that only the OWT FO UOY DNATS-REDNU.

SH-SH-SH—it's a secret!

EMOC NO DNA EVAH NUF!

"Secret method of communication" means sending your message so that only those who know the code will understand.

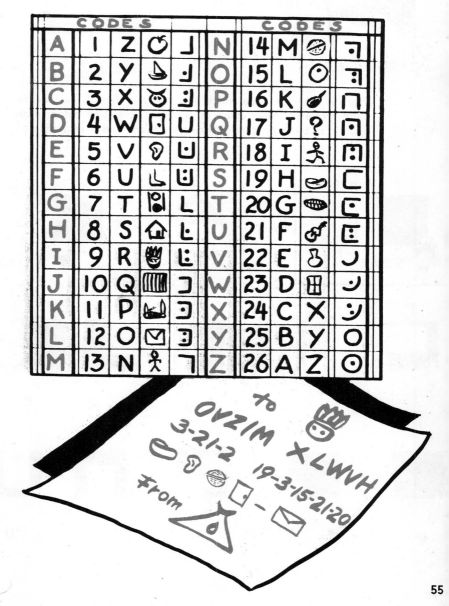

STRING — STRETCH TIGHT

A TIN CAN TELEPHONE

CARD SIGNALS

Here is a secret code which you and your friends can use to send messages clear across a room or yard. Cut out a large square of black or dark-colored cardboard and a rectangle of

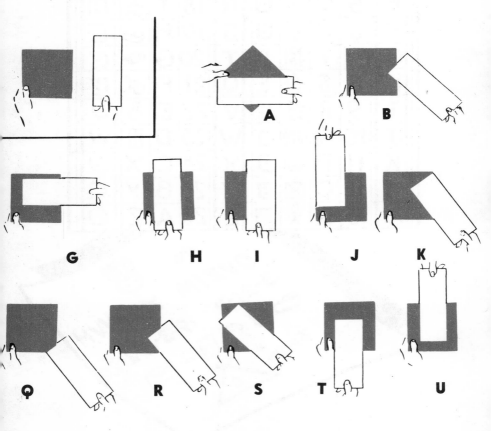

TIN CAN

BUTTON

white or light-colored cardboard. Put them together in shapes which appear as much like the letters as possible. The code alphabet is given below in full. Why not try it?

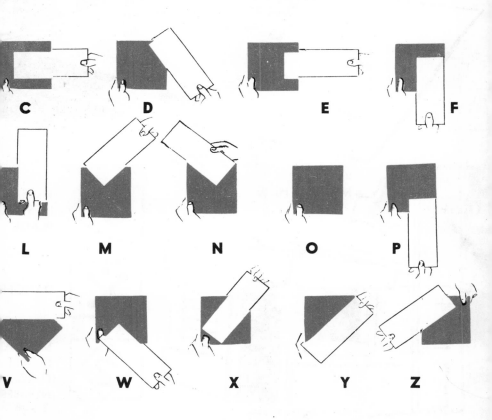

C   D   E   F

L   M   N   O   P

V   W   X   Y   Z

INVISIBLE INK

Invisible ink used by secret agents has fooled many a person. Try your hand at secret writing. With an ordinary school pen write on a plain sheet of paper. *But* instead of ink use milk or lemon juice. When it dries it becomes *invisible,* and your sheet of paper will be blank. To bring out the writing hold the sheet over a small flame — but not close enough to catch fire.

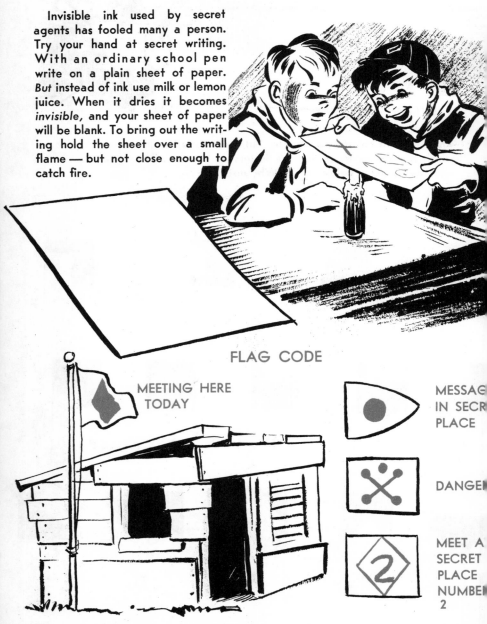

FLAG CODE

MEETING HERE TODAY

MESSAGE IN SECRET PLACE

DANGER

MEET AT SECRET PLACE NUMBER 2

MAKE BELIEVE

ELECTIVE 2

Each time you do one of the following things you receive *one credit*.

1. Take part in planning and putting on a Den skit, including (a) costumes (b) scenery (c) sound effects.

2. Make some scenery for a Den skit.

3. Make and operate the sound effects for a Den skit.

4. Be the narrator for a Den skit.

5. Make a paper sack mask for a character part.

MOTHER'S OR DAD'S INITIALS AND DATE FOR EACH CREDIT

⑤ 1964 C.T

SOUND EFFECTS

HORSES — Make "clop-clop" sound by pounding two hollow coconut halves on wooden board. _ _ _   _ _ _

RAIN — Roll peas in a pan.

BREAKING GLASS — Drop a box containing pieces of broken glass.

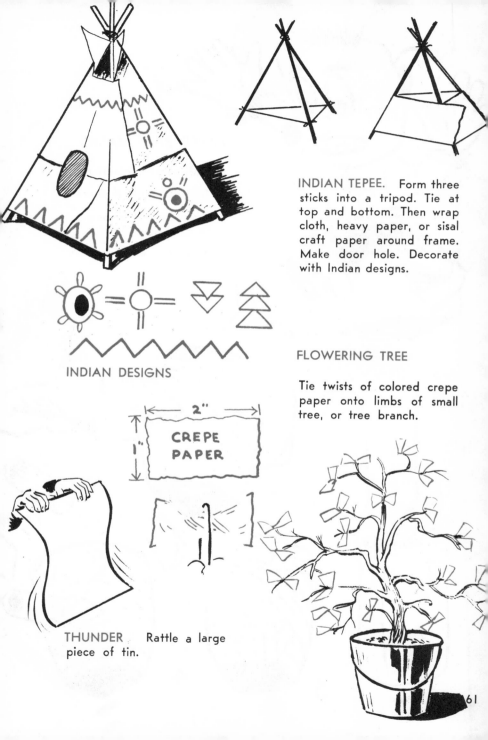

INDIAN TEPEE. Form three sticks into a tripod. Tie at top and bottom. Then wrap cloth, heavy paper, or sisal craft paper around frame. Make door hole. Decorate with Indian designs.

INDIAN DESIGNS

FLOWERING TREE

Tie twists of colored crepe paper onto limbs of small tree, or tree branch.

2"

1"

CREPE PAPER

THUNDER Rattle a large piece of tin.

61

PAPER BAG MASKS

1. Stuff paper bag with rags
2. Tie bag at top if desired
3. Paste strips over bag to give shape
4. Add nose, ears, etc.
5. Paint

HANDICRAFT

ELECTIVE 3

For each thing you make you receive *one credit*.

1. Make something useful.

MOTHER'S OR DAD'S INITIALS AND DATE FOR EACH CREDIT

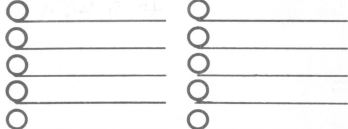

DOORSTOPS

BEAD

BUTTON

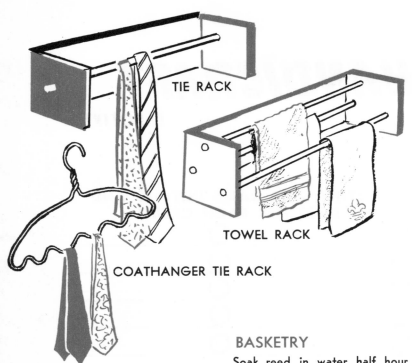

TIE RACK

TOWEL RACK

COATHANGER TIE RACK

BASKETRY

Soak reed in water half hour before weaving. Dip often during weaving to keep flexible.

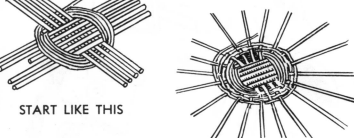

START LIKE THIS

SEPARATE SPOKES

FINISHED

RADIO

Each time you do this you get *one credit*.

1. Make and use a crystal set.

MOTHER'S OR DAD'S INITIALS AND
DATE FOR EACH CREDIT

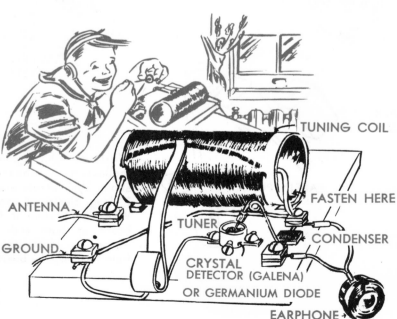

TUNING COIL

FASTEN HERE

ANTENNA

TUNER

CONDENSER

GROUND

CRYSTAL
DETECTOR (GALENA)
OR GERMANIUM DIODE

EARPHONE

Your dad can remember the first time he ever heard something on the radio. Maybe he listened over a crystal set. Ask him to tell you about it. Ask him what he heard and how it sounded. It's not very hard to make a crystal set if you follow the plans below. Ask your dad or some other grown-up to explain the plans to you.

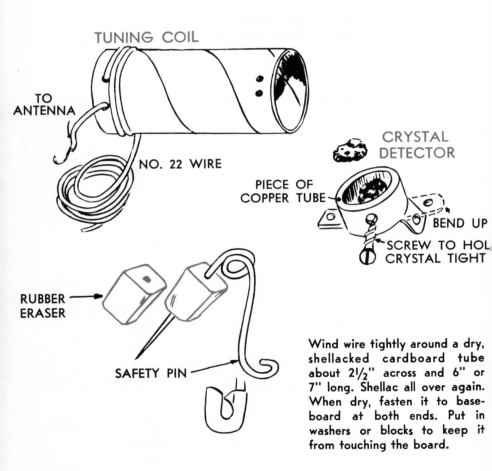

TUNING COIL

TO ANTENNA

NO. 22 WIRE

CRYSTAL DETECTOR

PIECE OF COPPER TUBE

BEND UP

SCREW TO HOL CRYSTAL TIGHT

RUBBER ERASER

SAFETY PIN

Wind wire tightly around a dry, shellacked cardboard tube about 2½" across and 6" or 7" long. Shellac all over again. When dry, fasten it to baseboard at both ends. Put in washers or blocks to keep it from touching the board.

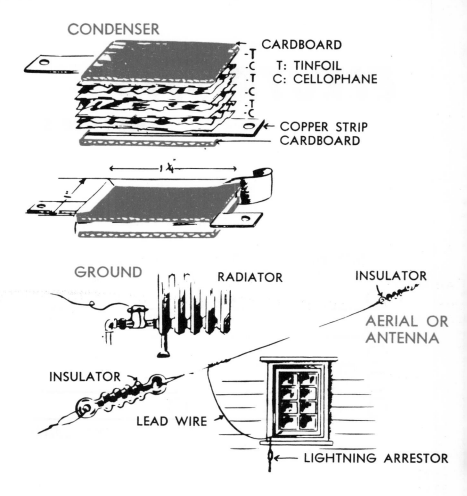

CONDENSER

CARDBOARD

T: TINFOIL
C: CELLOPHANE

COPPER STRIP
CARDBOARD

GROUND   RADIATOR   INSULATOR

AERIAL OR
ANTENNA

INSULATOR

LEAD WIRE

LIGHTNING ARRESTOR

The parts for a crystal set can be bought. One of these parts is a ready-made fixed condenser. But it's fun to make much of it yourself from scrap materials. The tuner is a strip of brass. One end is screwed down to the baseboard at such an angle that it can be turned with the other end sliding over the tuning coil in an arc. Scrape shellac and covering from wire along the tuner's path. The end of the ground wire, with covering scraped off, is fastened to a pipe driven into the ground. A radiator will do fine. The aerial can be put on the roof. Insulate it at both ends.

ELECTRICITY

ELECTIVE 5

Each time you do one of the following things you receive *one credit*.

1. Make a simple voltaic cell or a Leyden jar.

2. Wire a buzzer or doorbell or repair one.

3. Make an electric buzzer game.

MOTHER'S OR DAD'S INITIALS AND DATE FOR EACH CREDIT

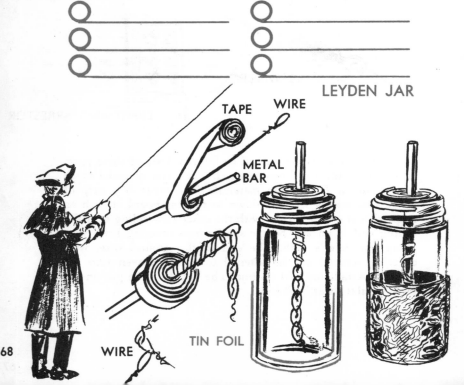

LEYDEN JAR

TAPE   WIRE

METAL BAR

TIN FOIL

WIRE

68

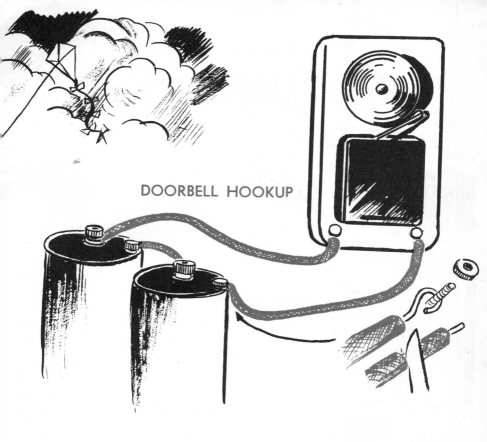

DOORBELL HOOKUP

This is another door into the wonder world. Get your dad to tell you the story of how Benjamin Franklin collected electricity in a Leyden jar by sending up a kite in a lightning storm. The discovery of electricity back in that day was almost as important as the breaking of the atom in ours.

Work with your dad in making a simple voltaic cell or a Leyden jar. Have him show you how to wire a buzzer or doorbell and have fun making up some electric buzzer games.

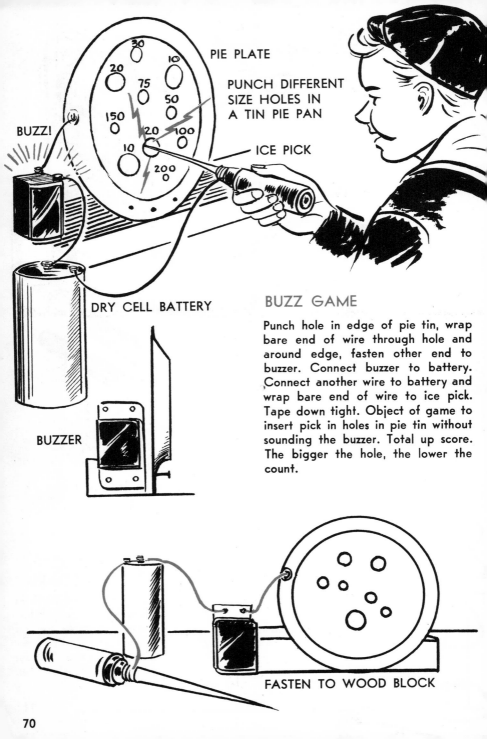

PIE PLATE

PUNCH DIFFERENT
SIZE HOLES IN
A TIN PIE PAN

30
20
10
75
50
150
20
100
BUZZ!
10
200

ICE PICK

DRY CELL BATTERY

BUZZER

BUZZ GAME

Punch hole in edge of pie tin, wrap
bare end of wire through hole and
around edge, fasten other end to
buzzer. Connect buzzer to battery.
Connect another wire to battery and
wrap bare end of wire to ice pick.
Tape down tight. Object of game to
insert pick in holes in pie tin without
sounding the buzzer. Total up score.
The bigger the hole, the lower the
count.

FASTEN TO WOOD BLOCK

70

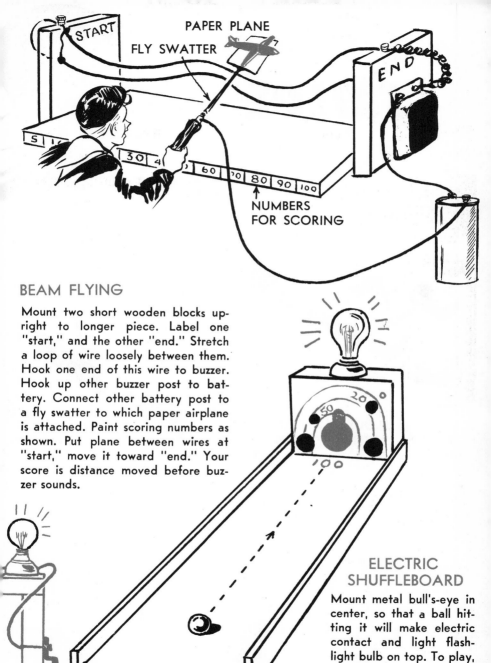

BEAM FLYING

Mount two short wooden blocks upright to longer piece. Label one "start," and the other "end." Stretch a loop of wire loosely between them. Hook one end of this wire to buzzer. Hook up other buzzer post to battery. Connect other battery post to a fly swatter to which paper airplane is attached. Paint scoring numbers as shown. Put plane between wires at "start," move it toward "end." Your score is distance moved before buzzer sounds.

ELECTRIC SHUFFLEBOARD

Mount metal bull's-eye in center, so that a ball hitting it will make electric contact and light flashlight bulb on top. To play, roll tennis ball up trough.

71

SAILOR

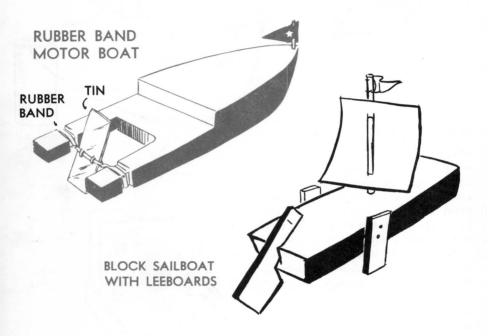

RUBBER BAND
MOTOR BOAT

RUBBER
BAND

TIN

BLOCK SAILBOAT
WITH LEEBOARDS

Each time you do one of the following, you receive *one credit*.

1. Make a model boat with rubber band or mechanical motor.
2. Make or put together a toy sailboat. Sail it.
3. Make a model shipyard.

MOTHER'S OR DAD'S INITIALS AND DATE FOR EACH CREDIT

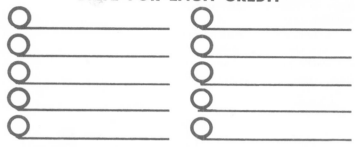

JET BOAT

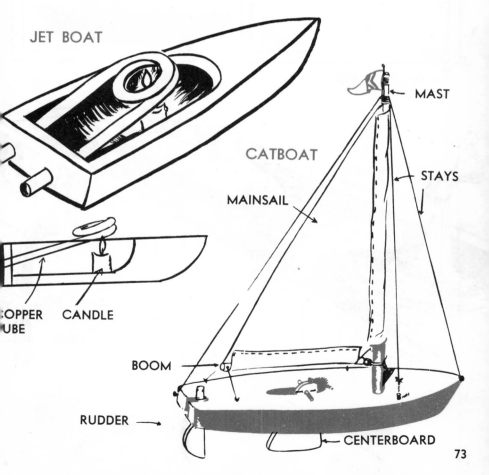

CATBOAT

MAST

STAYS

MAINSAIL

COPPER TUBE

CANDLE

BOOM

RUDDER

CENTERBOARD

73

DRY DOCK

Make tight wooden box. Seal joints with putty. Put hinged doors in center. Add rubber strips on center edges of doors for watertight fit. Add drain hose and clamp. To operate, fill with water, put boat in end with drain, close doors, open drain hose.

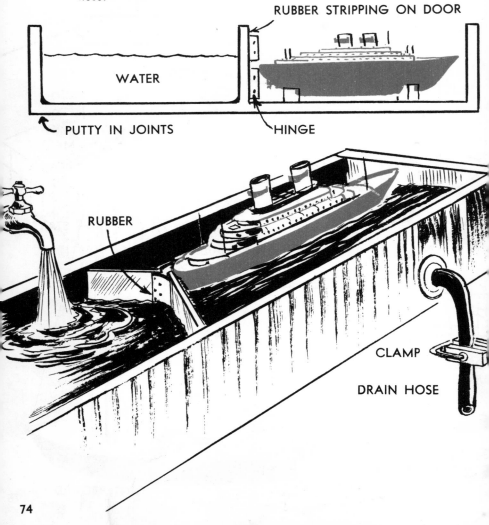

RUBBER STRIPPING ON DOOR

WATER

PUTTY IN JOINTS   HINGE

RUBBER

CLAMP

DRAIN HOSE

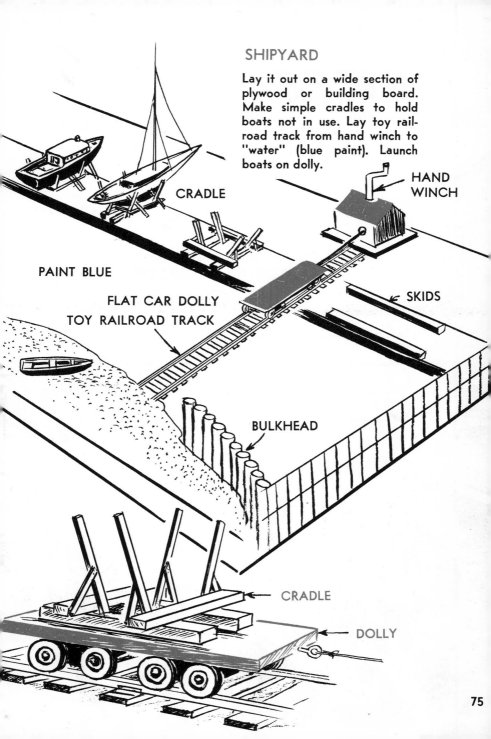

SHIPYARD

Lay it out on a wide section of plywood or building board. Make simple cradles to hold boats not in use. Lay toy railroad track from hand winch to "water" (blue paint). Launch boats on dolly.

HAND WINCH

CRADLE

PAINT BLUE

FLAT CAR DOLLY
TOY RAILROAD TRACK

SKIDS

BULKHEAD

CRADLE

DOLLY

KITES

Each time you do one of the following you receive *one credit*.

1. Make and fly a kite.

2. Make and fly a glider (not paper).

3. Make a model airport.

MOTHER'S OR DAD'S INITIALS AND DATE FOR EACH CREDIT

① _March 1965 C.H_

② _____

③ _____

④ _____

⑤ _____

○ _____

○ _____

○ _____

○ _____

○ _____

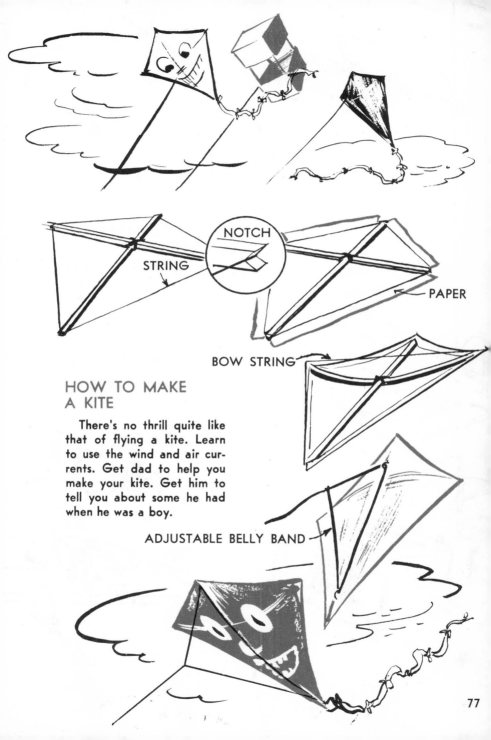

NOTCH

STRING

PAPER

BOW STRING

HOW TO MAKE A KITE

There's no thrill quite like that of flying a kite. Learn to use the wind and air currents. Get dad to help you make your kite. Get him to tell you about some he had when he was a boy.

ADJUSTABLE BELLY BAND

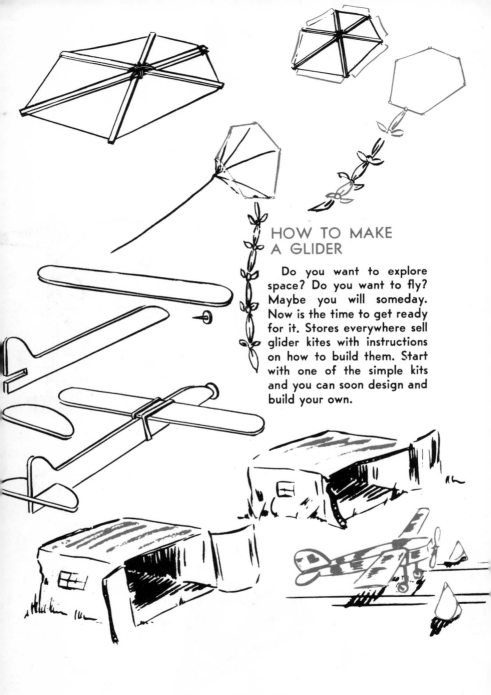

HOW TO MAKE
A GLIDER

Do you want to explore space? Do you want to fly? Maybe you will someday. Now is the time to get ready for it. Stores everywhere sell glider kites with instructions on how to build them. Start with one of the simple kits and you can soon design and build your own.

MODEL AIRPORT

Why not build your own airport for your gliders? The picture below shows you how. A wooden box serves as your control tower. Your flashlight beam through a piece of green glass is the signal "take off." A red light keeps the pilot grounded.

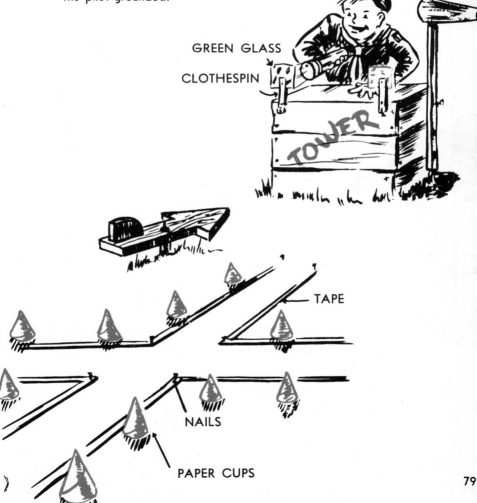

GREEN GLASS

CLOTHESPIN

TOWER

TAPE

NAILS

PAPER CUPS

FOOTPOWER

Each time you do one of the following things you receive *one credit*.

1. Make a pair of stilts and walk with them.
2. Make a pair of "puddle jumpers" and walk with them.
3. Make a roller and race with it.

MOTHER'S OR DAD'S INITIALS AND DATE FOR EACH CREDIT

ADJUSTABLE STILTS

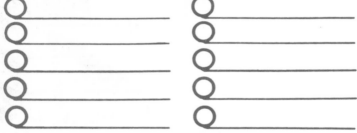

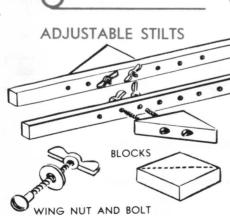

BLOCKS

WING NUT AND BOLT

Make a pair of stilts out of 1" x 2" lumber and a piece of 2" x 4".

Round off corners of 1" x 2" with sandpaper so the edges won't cut into your arms.

Foot rest 2" x 4" x 6". Cut across as shown.

Drill holes for 1/4" round head bolts.

Drill holes in leg 3" apart. Then you can raise or lower the foot rest.

Man travels on foot where machines and even horses cannot go—up steep mountains or up tall trees. So you want to learn to balance on your feet.

"PUDDLE JUMPER"

Punch two holes opposite each other in a tin can.

Loop "clothes rope." Put ends through holes and tie a large knot in the end of each rope.

Put foot on can. Draw rope up snug.

Make a pair and walk on them. Get dad to make a pair and have a walking race with him. Ropes should be fixed so you pull on them as you walk.

MAKE A ROLLER AND RACE WITH IT

Nail two light sticks together. Wood laths or trellis sticks are the right size—¼″ x 1¼″ x 30″. The roller is an old buggy or tricycle wheel.

To start, hold end of stick in right hand with bottom end on walk slanted away from in front of you. Set wheel on top of stick and let it roll down shaft to sidewalk. Now keep the wheel going by running along behind it and lightly pushing the cross piece against it. You'll learn to steer the wheel by turning your cross piece to left or right. With practice you can turn it around and come back.

You'll have lots of fun running races with your roller.

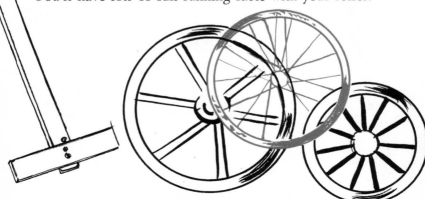

MACHINES

Each time you do one of the following things you receive *one credit*.

1. Tell the names and models of ten different automobiles or trucks as they go by at a distance of about fifty feet.

2. Find out from dad or some other adult what the dashboard instruments of a car show, and be able to tell when something is wrong.

3. Make or put together a model automobile.

MOTHER'S OR DAD'S INITIALS AND DATE FOR EACH CREDIT

① *1964 C.H*

OIL   Shows pressure of oil in engine.

TEMPERATURE   Shows temperature of water in radiator.
Warns you if engine is running hot.

GAS   Shows amount of gasoline in tank.

AMPS   Shows "amperage" (electricity). Tells whether
your battery is charging or discharging.

SPEED   Shows how fast you are going in miles per hour.

When you're out some day with your dad and mother, you can play a little game. See who can be first to name the automobiles that pass you on the way. Every time you name one first and name it correctly you score a point. After you have played the game for a little while you will find you've probably earned a credit in Machines.

Why not make a model of the car you like best? You can carve one out of soap or make one from a model kit. You may want to design your own super rocket car.

1950 FORD

1940 DODGE

1931 PIERCE ARROW

1920 CHEVROLET

1911 CADILLAC

1901 PACKARD

HOW CARS
HAVE CHANGED

PARTIES AND GIFTS

ELECTIVE 10

Each time you do one of the following you receive *one credit*.

1. Make a gift or toy for someone and give it to him.
2. Help to prepare for a home party.

MOTHER'S OR DAD'S INITIALS AND
DATE FOR EACH CREDIT

O *C. H. 1964*
O
O
O
O

O
O
O
O
O

It's lots of fun to have a party when you help plan it and help get ready for it. You can set the table and arrange the chairs. You can help plan the games and get the things together needed for the games or help with the dusting or run the sweeper. Parties are fun when every one helps.

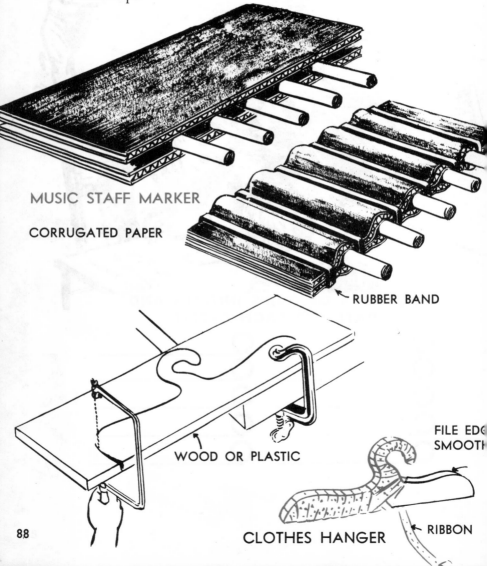

MUSIC STAFF MARKER

CORRUGATED PAPER

← RUBBER BAND

WOOD OR PLASTIC

FILE EDG
SMOOTH

CLOTHES HANGER

← RIBBON

We usually give gifts at special times—for birthdays, Christmas, Mother's Day, or Father's Day. But you don't have to wait for one of these special times to make something for a friend or a member of the family. A Cub Scout gives good will, so pick out somebody and make something for him or her. Your parents and your Den leaders can help you get some ideas.

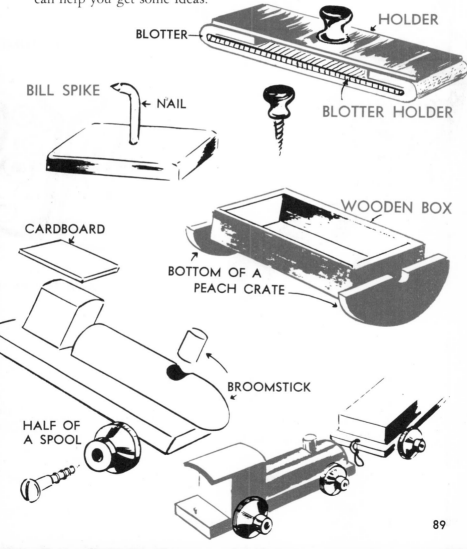

HOLDER

BLOTTER

BLOTTER HOLDER

BILL SPIKE

← NAIL

CARDBOARD

WOODEN BOX

BOTTOM OF A PEACH CRATE

BROOMSTICK

HALF OF A SPOOL

INDIANS

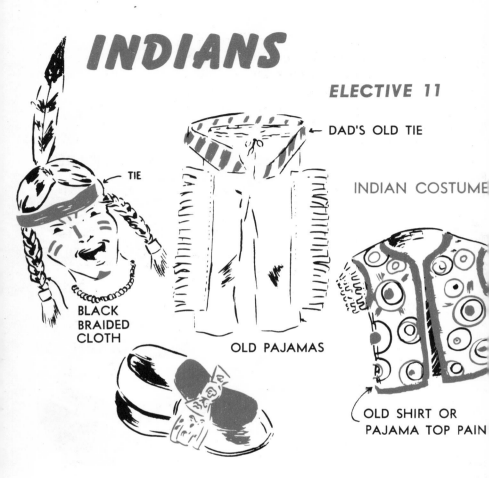

← DAD'S OLD TIE

INDIAN COSTUME

TIE

BLACK
BRAIDED
CLOTH

OLD PAJAMAS

OLD SHIRT OR
PAJAMA TOP PAIN

Each time you do one of the following things you receive *one credit*.

1. Make one part of an Indian costume.
2. Take part in an Indian dance.
3. Make an Indian weapon such as a tomahawk or spear.
4. Make an Indian shield.

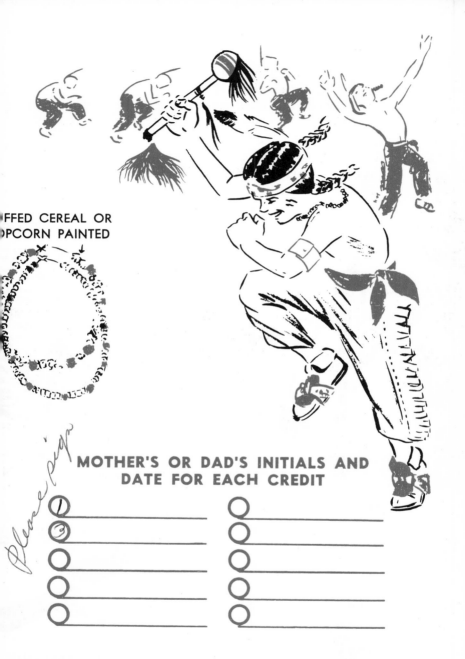

FFED CEREAL OR
PCORN PAINTED

MOTHER'S OR DAD'S INITIALS AND DATE FOR EACH CREDIT

Many boys wish they might have been Indians. Do you? If you do, can you tell why?

It's because of all the things the Indians did. Those who lived on the plains were good horsemen. Those who lived in the woods were hunters. They could shoot straight with a bow. They could make all kinds of things.

Well, of course you can't really be an Indian. But Cub Scouts can do lots of things Indians did. Just look at all the interesting things below. They are all fun, and they are real Indian things.

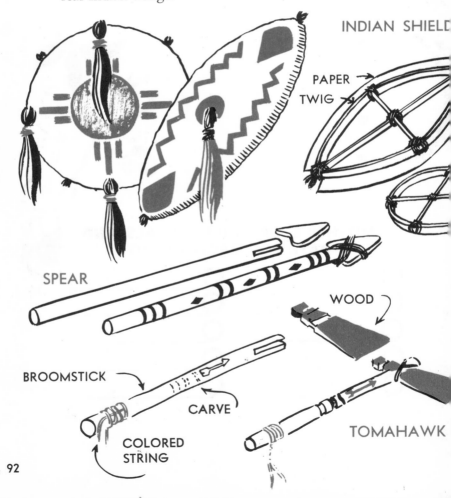

INDIAN SHIELD

PAPER

TWIG

SPEAR

WOOD

BROOMSTICK

CARVE

COLORED STRING

TOMAHAWK

SONGS

Each time you do one of the following you receive *one credit*.

1. Learn and sing the first and last stanzas of the "Star-Spangled Banner" and "America." (You may do this only once.)

2. Learn the words and sing three Cub Scout songs.

3. Learn the words and sing the first stanza of three familiar hymns.

Please Sign

MOTHER'S OR DAD'S INITIALS AND DATE FOR EACH CREDIT

1 ○ _____   ○ _____
2 ○ _____   ○ _____
3 ○ _____   ○ _____
○ _____   ○ _____
○ _____   ○ _____

PAPER AND COMB KAZOO

Hold paper loosely on comb — Hum on it.

THE STAR-SPANGLED BANNER

O, say! can you see, by the dawn's early light,
What so proudly we hailed at the twilight's last gleaming?
Whose broad stripes and bright stars, thru' the perilous fight,
O'er the ramparts we watched, were so gallantly streaming.
  And the rockets' red glare, the bombs bursting in air,
  Gave proof thru' the night that our flag was still there.
Oh, say! does that Star-Spangled Banner yet wave
O'er the land of the free and the home of the brave?

O, thus be it ever when free men shall stand
Between their loved homes and the war's desolation!
Blest with vict'ry and peace, may the heav'n rescued land
Praise the Pow'r that hath made and preserved us a nation!
  Then conquer we must, when our cause it is just,
  And this be our motto: "In God Is Our Trust!"
And the Star-Spangled Banner in triumph shall wave
O'er the land of the free and the home of the brave!

FRANCIS SCOTT KEY

AMERICA

First Stanza	*Second Stanza*
My country, 'tis of thee,	Our fathers' God, to Thee,
Sweet land of liberty,	Author of liberty,
Of thee I sing;	To thee we sing;
Land where my fathers died!	Long may our land be bright
Land of the Pilgrim's pride!	With freedom's holy light;
From ev'ry mountain side,	Protect us by Thy might,
Let freedom ring!	Great God, our King!

CUB SCOUT SONGS

I HAVE A DOG
(To tune of "Reuben, Reuben, I've Been Thinking")
I have a dog, his name is Fido,
I have raised him from a pup.
He can stand upon his hind legs
If you hold his front legs up.

TRAIN SONG
(To tune of "Yankee Doodle")

I met an engine on a hill,
All hot and broken-hearted,
And this is what he said to me
As up the hill he started:

(Slowly)
I think I can, I think I can,
At any rate I'll try.
I think I can, I think I can
At any rate I'll try.

He reached the top, and looking back
To where he stood and doubted,
He started on the downward track
And this is what he shouted:

(Faster)
I knew I could, I knew I could,
I never should have doubted.
I knew I could, I knew I could,
I never should have doubted.

CUB SCOUTING WE WILL GO
(To tune of "Jingle Bells")

Cub Scouting we will go
To a Den where we can play;
Sunshine, rain or snow,
Happy on our way.
As buddies we will greet
Faces gleaming bright;
What fun it is when we can
meet
And do the things we like!

Chorus
Cub Scout Days!
Cub Scout Days!
Dear old Cub Scout days!
O, what fun for everyone
In a Den where we can play, O!
(Repeat Chorus)

Do you sing Cub Scout songs in your Den meetings and Pack meetings? Maybe you can lead your Den in singing three Cub Scout songs at your next meeting. They will sound better if you sing them quietly.

Did you ever go to a meeting or a program where "The Star-Spangled Banner" was sung? Did you know the words? Even some big folks haven't learned the words of our national song. You can be a better Cub Scout and a better American if you learn them.

GOOD NIGHT CUB SCOUTS
(Tune: "Good Night, Ladies")

Good night, Cub Scouts.
Good night, Cub Scouts.
Good night, Cub Scouts,
We're going to leave you now.

Merrily, we Cub along, Cub along, Cub along,
Merrily, we Cub along,
Up the Cub Scout trail.

Sweet dreams, Cub Scouts.
Sweet dreams, Cub Scouts.
Sweet dreams, Cub Scouts,
We're going to leave you now.

BE GAME, BE SQUARE
(Tune: "My Bonnie Lies Over the Ocean")

Cub Scouts, we will always be happy,
Be loyal, be game, and be square;
And soon by our work and endeavor,
Be Lions or Wolves or Bears.
    Be Game—Be Square—
    Do our best wherever we go, we go,
    Be Game—Be Square—
    Give Good Will wherever we go.

I KNOW A LITTLE PUSSY
(Tune: Sing each line a note higher in scale;
sing "meows" down scale.)

I know a little pussy,   She'll always be a pussy,
Her coat is silver gray.   She'll never be a cat,
She lives out in the meadow,   For she's a pussy willow.
She'll never run away.   Now, what do you think of that?
    Meow, meow, meow, meow, meow, meow, meow, meow,
    SCAT!

DRAWING

Each time you do one of the following things you receive *one credit*.

1. Make a freehand sketch.
2. Make a strip of at least three cartoons.
3. Draw, paint, or crayon some scenery for a Den or Pack skit.
4. Make a stencil pattern.
5. Fix up your own room with mother's and dad's help and permission.

You can't tell whether you can draw a picture until you try. Don't expect the first one to be too good. Keep trying. Some of the pictures on the next page will show you how to start.

If you make some cartoons, try to think up your own cartoon people instead of taking them from the newspaper. Maybe you can make up a little story about a Cub Scout or a dog.

Please this

MOTHER'S OR DAD'S INITIALS AND DATE FOR EACH CREDIT

Build your drawings around circles, ovals, squares and other shapes. Fill in the details last.

99

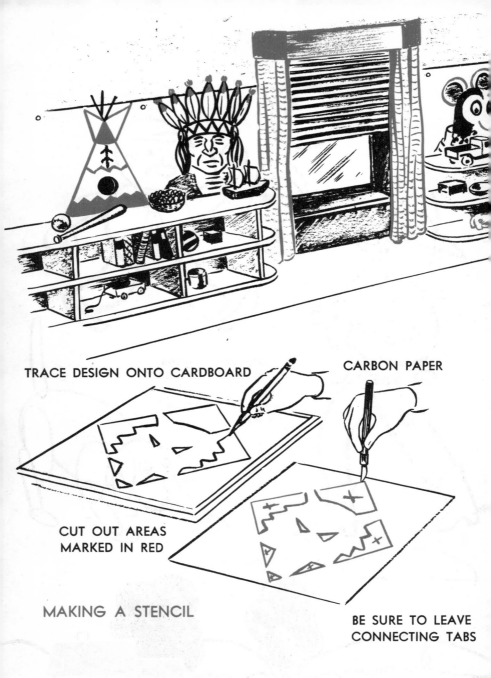

TRACE DESIGN ONTO CARDBOARD

CARBON PAPER

CUT OUT AREAS
MARKED IN RED

MAKING A STENCIL

BE SURE TO LEAVE
CONNECTING TABS

DECORATE YOUR ROOM

Cover lower part of wall with heavy wrapping paper. (Use thumb tacks to hold it in place.) Paste, draw, or paint on your favorite animals, Indians, etc.

LAY STENCIL OVER PAPER. PAINT OVER CUT-OUT AREAS

HOW TO DRAW A WOLF, BEAR, OR LION

Draw a diamond for wolf, a circle for bear or lion.

Then add lines as shown.

PHOTOGRAPHY

ELECTIVE 14

Each time you do this you receive *one credit*.

1. Make six prints from family negatives and put them in a homemade album. Label each picture.

MOTHER'S OR DAD'S INITIALS AND DATE FOR EACH CREDIT

O _____   O _____

O _____   O _____

O _____   O _____

O _____   O _____

O _____   O _____

You will want to start a picture album of your own when you see how easy it is to print good pictures. Examine the negatives carefully and see if you can tell which ones will make good prints and which ones are over-exposed or under-exposed.

Ask your mother or dad or some grownup to help you read the new words about photography.

STICKY TAPE

PRINTING PAPER

NEGATIVE

HOLE

GLASS

BOX

100 WATT LIGHT

RED LIGHT

WOOD OR CARDBOARD

FIXING BATH NEXT

DEVELOPER FIRST

WOOD

PRINTING A NEGATIVE

In room lit only by red light, place negative rough side up over glass in light box. Place printing paper over negative. Hold in place with tape and board. Turn on light in box. After exposure, remove printing paper and put in developer first, then in fixing bath.

SNAPSHOT ALBUM

BIRDS

Each time you do one of the following things you receive *one credit*.

1. Make a list of all the birds you see in a week.

2. Point out ten different kinds of birds.

3. Put out nesting material (yarn, string) for birds and tell what birds use it.

4. Feed wild birds for a week and tell what birds you attract.

5. Read a book about wild birds.

6. Know three birds by their songs.

MOTHER'S OR DAD'S INITIALS AND DATE FOR EACH CREDIT

Whether you live in an apartment or a house in the city or in the country, you can have fun with birds. If you live in the city there is probably a park nearby where you can watch and feed birds. In the country, birds will be all around you.

There are many different kinds of birds, and they live in different kinds of places. You will see some birds hopping across the ground. Others will be in bushes or trees. Still others will swim in the water or fly overhead. Take along a notebook when you go out and write down what you see birds doing and what they look like. Then you can find their names in a bird book.

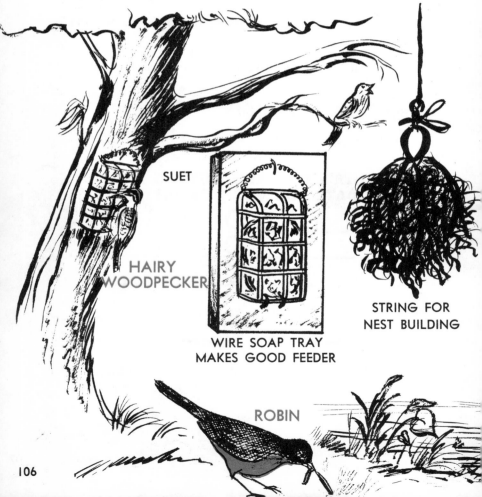

SUET

HAIRY WOODPECKER

WIRE SOAP TRAY MAKES GOOD FEEDER

STRING FOR NEST BUILDING

ROBIN

KILLDEER
Usually found around water. Nests on the ground. Cries "Killdee! Killdee!" when alarmed.

MOURNING DOVE
Large grayish bird, sometimes called "wild pigeon." Call—"coo, coo, coo."

SCREECH OWL
Small owl with "horns." Nests in holes in trees. Flies at night.

CROW
Large, all black bird seen in woods and around farms. Call—"caw, caw, caw."

CATBIRD
Gray bird, a little smaller than a robin. Nests in bushes. Call sounds like a cat— "mew, mew, mew."

MALLARD

107

FLICKER
A brownish woodpecker, larger than a robin. Feeds on ground and in trees. Nests in holes in trees.

KINGBIRD
A bold member of the flycatcher family. Feeds on mosquitoes and many other insects.

ORIOLE'S NEST

ROBIN'S NEST

SPARROW'S NEST

THRUSH'S NEST

WINDOW
FEEDING
STATION

HANGING FEEDER
2 x 2 BLOCK
HANG FROM TREE.
PUT SUET IN HOLES.

WHAT TO FEED BIRDS

Sparrow, juncoes—chicken feed, cracked corn, millet.
Cowbirds, bluejays—sunflower seeds, peanuts, nut meats.
Chickadees, cardinals—bread crumbs, stale doughnuts.
Woodpeckers, nuthatches, creepers—suet, meat fats, peanut butter.

SOME GOOD BIRD BOOKS

All About Birds, Robert S. Lemmon (Random House, New York, N. Y.).

Amazing Book of Birds, The, Hilda Simon (Hart Publishing Co., New York, N. Y.).

Audubon Bird Leaflets (National Audubon Society, 1130 Fifth Avenue, New York 28, N. Y.).

Birds, Golden Nature Guides, Zim and Gabrielson (Simon and Schuster, New York, N. Y.).

First Book of Birds, The, Margaret Williamson (Franklin Watts Inc., 699 Madison Ave., New York 21, N. Y.).

1001 Questions About Birds, Alan and Helen Cruickshank (Dodd Mead and Co., New York, N. Y.).

PETS

Each time you do one of these things you get *one credit*.
1. Keep an animal pet.
2. Tell how to treat strange dogs.
3. Read a book about a pet animal.

MOTHER'S OR DAD'S INITIALS AND DATE FOR EACH CREDIT

① 1964 C.H.	○	
① 1964 C.H.	○	
○	○	
○	○	
○	○	

SMALL ANIMAL CAGE

GLASS TERRARIUM

FISH BOWL

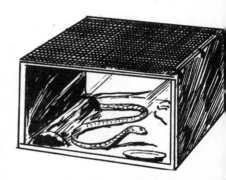

TERRARIUM WITH SCREEN TOP

RABBIT HUTCH

WHAT TO FEED YOUR PETS

Dog or cat—Prepared dog or cat food. Table scraps. Water.

Birds—Bird seed. Grit. Water.

Rabbit—Prepared pellets. Water. Carrots, lettuce, clover.

Turtle—Prepared turtle food. Insects. Small bits of meat. Water.

Snake—Insects. Small bits of meat. Water.

Fish—Prepared fish foods.
Land snails—Lettuce, cabbage, celery leaves.

White mice or rats—Prepared food. Nuts. Seeds. (Pet shops and many food markets sell ready prepared food for pets.)

All boys like dogs. Sometimes we like them so well that we do the wrong things with strange dogs. You can do lots of things with your own dog or the dog next door. These same things you wouldn't want to do with a dog you knew nothing about. You wouldn't understand him and he wouldn't understand you. There are a few rules for you to remember when you see strange dogs.

1. Don't handle them.
2. Don't move too quickly near them.
3. Never try to scare them away.
4. Never show that you fear them.
5. Never run away from them; walk quietly away.

Wherever you live you can keep some kind of an animal pet. Dogs, cats, rabbits, white mice or rats, canaries, parakeets, goldfish or tropical fish, turtles, snails, snakes, chickens, ducks, farm animals, or even insects such as praying mantis or crickets all make interesting pets.

GARDENER

Each time you do one of the following things you receive *one credit*.

1. Plant and raise a box garden.
2. Grow a sweet potato vine indoors.
3. Make a terrarium.
4. Plant and raise a vegetable garden.

CORN — 2 FT.
BUSH LIMA BEANS — 2 FT.
ONIONS — 1 FT.
CARROTS — 1 FT.
BEETS — 2 FT. → CABBAGE

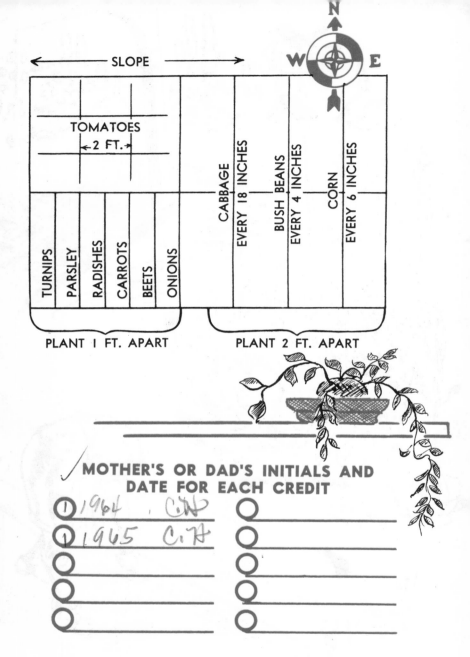

SLOPE

N
W E

TOMATOES
← 2 FT. →

TURNIPS | PARSLEY | RADISHES | CARROTS | BEETS | ONIONS

CABBAGE

BUSH BEANS | EVERY 18 INCHES

EVERY 4 INCHES

CORN | EVERY 6 INCHES

PLANT 1 FT. APART

PLANT 2 FT. APART

MOTHER'S OR DAD'S INITIALS AND DATE FOR EACH CREDIT

- ① 1964   C.N
- ① 1965   C.H
- ○
- ○
- ○

- ○
- ○
- ○
- ○
- ○

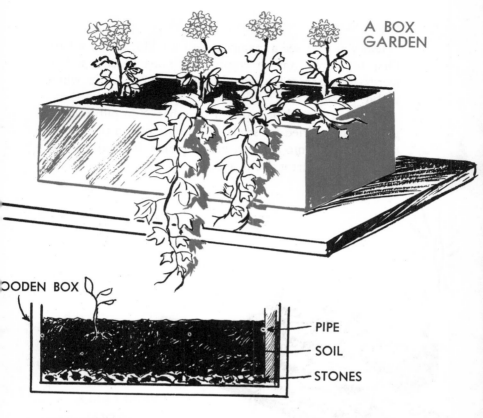

A BOX
GARDEN

OODEN BOX

PIPE

SOIL

STONES

A TERRARIUM

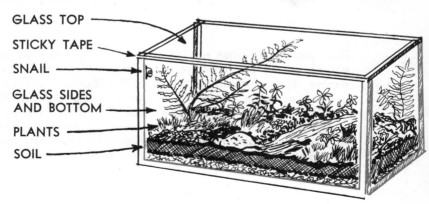

GLASS TOP

STICKY TAPE

SNAIL

GLASS SIDES
AND BOTTOM

PLANTS

SOIL

Did you ever see a magician pull a rabbit out of a hat? First he shows you an empty hat. Then he says a few words, waves a magic wand, and pulls out a big white rabbit.

Growing a garden is almost like that. You put into the ground some dried up seeds, and in almost no time at all they've turned into healthy, grown plants. It's really magic to get a big carrot from a seed so tiny you can hardly see it.

NORTH

SOUTH

YOUR
VEGETABLE
GARDEN

Plant your garden rows running as nearly north and south as possible so the plants will get a lot of sun. If the ground is sloping, the rows should run crosswise. This is called "contour" planting as shown above. If the rows run up and down hill, rain will wash away the soil. This is called "erosion." The pictures on the two pages before this show you how far apart to space your rows. Plant smaller vegetables like beets and carrots so that they will not be in the shade of taller ones.

FOREST AND PLANT LIFE
CONSERVATION

Each time you do one of the following things you receive *one credit.*

1. Make a chart of pictures showing a few things you use every day that come from trees—table, chair, pencil, baseball bat, skis, wagon, fish pole, sled.

2. Make a collection of leaves from five trees that provide you with something useful.

3. Plant some grass seed on a patch of bare ground.

4. Carry out an experiment that shows how plants protect the soil.

5. Make a collection of five different kinds of wood used for lumber, boxes, and other useful things.

MOTHER'S OR DAD'S INITIALS AND DATE FOR EACH CREDIT

3 / 965 : C.½   O _____

3 / 964 . C ¾   O _____

O _____   O _____

O _____   O _____

O _____   O _____

Everyday, whatever you do, you use things that come from trees or other plants. They are very important to you. You can find pictures in old magazines and newspapers that show all the things that are made from wood, or that wood is used for. You can find small pieces of wood near carpentry shops, lumber yards, or new houses that are being built. Ask the man in charge to let you collect odds and ends.

SOME USEFUL TREES

PINE
Tall straight evergreen. Has cones, widely used for lumber.

SPRUCE
Member of pine order. Used in making paper.

MAPLE
Beautiful shade tree. We get maple sugar and valuable wood from it.

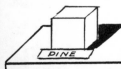

LEAF COLLECTION
MOUNT YOUR LEAVES
IN A SCRAPBOOK
WITH STICKY TAPE

WHITE PINE

BLUE SPRUCE

RED GUM

RED OAK

SUGAR MAPLE

...AK
big, sturdy hardwood.
...as acorns. Makes fine,
...ng-lasting lumber.

RED GUM
Sometimes called Sweet
Gum.
Juice good.

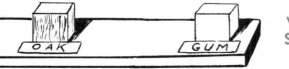

WOOD
SAMPLES

RUN-OFF PLOT

Sprinkle the same amount of water on each box, and collect the water that runs off in jars. Look carefully at the water in the jars. See how muddy the water is that ran off the bare soil? This shows how plants protect soil and keep it from washing away.

COOKING

Each time you do one of the following things you receive *one credit.*

1. Fix your own breakfast with at least one hot dish. Wash and put away the dishes.

2. Help fix at least one meal for the family. (Help set the table, cook the food, and wash the dishes.)

3. Help make an orangeade, lemonade, or hot chocolate drink for the family.

4. Cook satisfactorily something you haven't cooked before.

5. Help make and serve a gelatin dessert.

② 1965 C. N

③ 1965 C. N

Mother can help you most with cooking. Ask her to read this with you.

Start your cooking a little at a time. When you get your own breakfast, instead of cooking some fancy dish just boil an egg. There is even a trick in doing that, if you get it just right. You might have to try it several times to find out the right length of time. Don't forget, part of the bargain is to clean up the dishes after you get through.

The first time you cook something outdoors, try something like roasting "hot dogs" on a stick. You will find that it is best to let your fire burn down to coals instead of trying to cook in the flame.

HOW TO ROAST POTATOES

Wash and dry potatoes. Bury them deep in the hot ashes of a campfire and cover with hot coals. In about forty minutes test them by sticking a sharp sliver into them. If still hard, roast longer. Eat as soon as potatoes are done.

HOW TO MAKE GELATIN DESSERT

Add gelatin to amount of hot (not boiling) water shown on box. Stir until gelatin is dissolved. Allow to cool. Then put in ice box to harden.

HOW TO MAKE LEMONADE AND ORANGEADE

For every glass of ade you want, squeeze the juice of ½ lemon or orange. Add 2 teaspoons of sugar for lemonade, ½ teaspoon for orangeade—more if you like it sweeter. Stir well with 1 cup of water. Add ice to chill.

HOW TO ROAST A "HOT DOG"

Stick the "hot dog" on the sharp ends of a forked branch. Turn over the hot coals of a low fire until brown. Serve inside a roll (also toasted on the end of a stick) with relish or mustard.

HOW TO MAKE A STEW

Cut beef, veal or lamb into small pieces. Rub into a mixture of flour, salt and pepper. Place this in a pot and just cover meat with water. Let this simmer over fire for at least an hour. (Water should not boil hard.) Then add potatoes, carrots, onions and other vegetables. Cook until all contents are just tender.

OUTING

Family picnics, fishing trips, and Den outings give you a chance for great adventure if you help plan for them.

Each time you do one of the following things you receive *one credit*.

1. With your dad or another adult plan and take a fishing trip.

2. Help plan and run a picnic with your family.

3. Help plan and run a Den outing.

4. Assist in planning and laying out a treasure hunt, an obstacle race, or an adventure trail.

MOTHER'S OR DAD'S INITIALS AND
DATE FOR EACH CREDIT

- 1964. C.H
- 1964. C.H
- 1964 C.H
- 1963 C.H
-
-
-
-
-
-

If you help plan a Den outing, a good thing to start with is an obstacle race. It's something like "Follow-the-Leader." Think up a lot of funny things to crawl through or climb over and then see who can do it the fastest.

OBSTACLE RACE

BRIDGE

RIVER

TREASURE HUNT

SWIMMING

Each time you do one of the following things you receive *one credit* but you may earn a credit in each only once.

1. Float in water without touching bottom. Stay as motionless as you can for two minutes.

2. Swim on stomach or side, using any stroke you choose, for thirty feet.

3. Swim, using the backstroke, for thirty feet.

4. Jump into water feet first and swim fifty feet, any style.

Note: Be sure you always have with you a grownup who can swim.

There is something about this elective different from any other. That is: *Whenever you are working on your swimming, be sure that you always have with you a grownup who can swim.*

You get one credit for doing each of the things on the next page. *But you may earn a credit in each thing only once for Wolf Arrow Points.*

BACK FLOAT

Stretch your arms to the side and lie back on the water, letting your feet float up. Hold a deep breath. Keep your chest high. Let your head fall back until your ears are under water. This is a good way to rest in the water. Go at it slowly, easily.

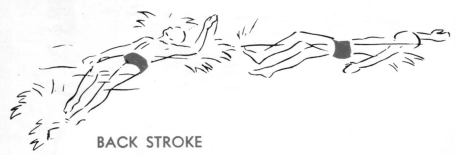

BACK STROKE

Use a flutter kick. Swing your arms in a smooth, even motion. Move them up out of the water, elbows bent, back over your head; and then straight down under your body. Have your palm turned to scoop the water. Your face stays above water so you can breathe in and out as you like.

SIDE STROKE

The side stroke is easy. You can swim on either side. At the end of each stroke your arms and legs are still, as shown in this side view, while you glide.

To start each stroke, draw your knees up and open your legs slowly. Draw your top knee up toward your chin. Draw your bottom foot well up behind you.

Stroke downward with your lower arm. Bring it up to join finger tips with your upper hand as shown.

Here is a top view of the position shown in the second picture. Note that the upper leg is brought forward.

Now bring your legs together with a strong scissors stroke. At the same time, reach ahead with your lower hand and push backward with the upper. You finish full stroke as in this top view.

SAFETY SERVICE

Each time you do one of these things, you get *one credit*.

1. If boys your age can, serve on the Safety Patrol in your school for two months while you are a Wolf.

2. Look over your home and, with dad, fix up unsafe things.

MOTHER'S OR DAD'S INITIALS AND DATE FOR EACH CREDIT

○ 1965 C·H

○ _____   ○ _____

○ _____   ○ _____

○ _____   ○ _____

○ _____   ○ _____

○ _____   ○ _____

In some schools boys of Cub Scout age can serve on the Safety Patrol. It's fine if you can do it for your school.

Maybe you have made a home safety inspection. But it is important to do it again because new dangers come along from time to time. They won't be found unless you look for them often. The picture on page 136 will help you make your inspection. Do it with your dad. You may need his help in getting rid of the dangers you find.

Besides the things shown, here are some other unsafe things to look for:

Holes or wrinkles in rugs and carpets, which will cause
   people to trip and fall. Small rugs on slippery floors.
Matches, poison, knives and other dangerous things
   within reach of small children.
Oily rags and other rubbish left around.

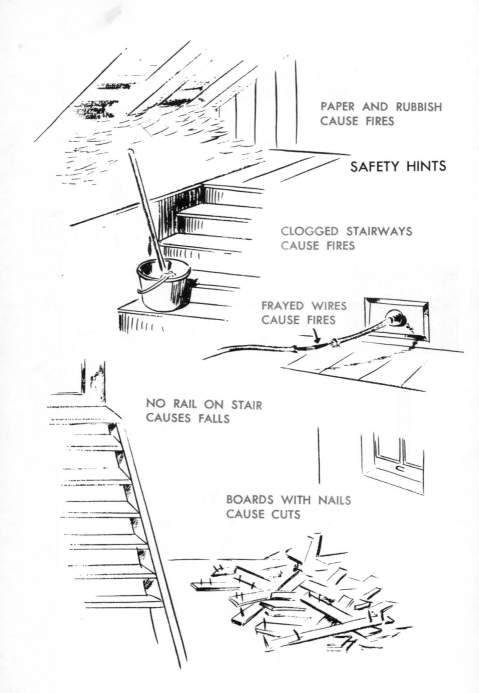

PAPER AND RUBBISH
CAUSE FIRES

SAFETY HINTS

CLOGGED STAIRWAYS
CAUSE FIRES

FRAYED WIRES
CAUSE FIRES

NO RAIL ON STAIR
CAUSES FALLS

BOARDS WITH NAILS
CAUSE CUTS

SPORTS

You will find six sports listed below. You may already have done a lot in some of them. If you have never been interested in sports, you will have fun in them now.

You receive one credit for doing each of these sports. *But you may earn a credit in each sport only once for Wolf Arrow Points.*

1. In tennis, show serving, scoring, and fault rules for singles. Play a set with dad, mother, brother, Den Chief, or another Cub Scout.

2. In baseball, show that you can play at least three positions, and take part in two full games.

3. Boating. (Know how to swim.) Show forward strokes, turn, and backstrokes. Row a boat around a 150-yard course set by your dad. Always have some grownup with you.

4. In archery, know the safety rules. Know how to shoot correctly. Put four of six arrows into a four-foot target fifty feet away.

5. In skiing know the skier's code. Demonstrate walking and kick turn, climbing with side step or herringbone, snowplow stop, stem turn, and show how to recover from a fall.

6. In ice skating know the safety rules. Skate at least 150 feet without falling and come to a complete stop.

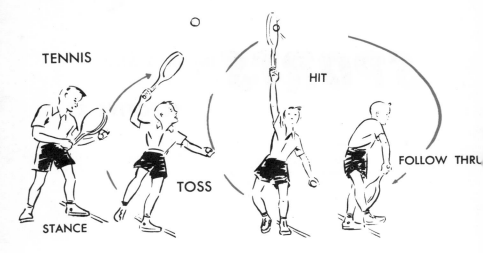

TENNIS

HIT

FOLLOW THRU

TOSS

STANCE

HOW TO SCORE

The player who wins the first point scores 15. For the next point, his score is 30. For the third point his score is 40. On the fourth point he scores game—UNLESS the other player has scored 40. When both players have scored 40, the score is called deuce. Whoever wins the next point scores advantage. If he wins the next point too, he scores game. But if the other player wins that last point, the score goes back to deuce. In other words, to win the game, a player must win two points in a row after deuce. The first player who wins six games wins a set, UNLESS the other player has won five games. With the game score five-to-five, one player must win two games ahead of the other for set.

HOW TO SERVE

Stand sideways to net, behind the base line, your left shoulder pointing in the direction of your target across the net. "Wind up" by lifting your racket in a circular motion behind you. Toss the ball straight up in front of your right shoulder. Toss it just in time and high enough to meet your racket at the top of its path well above your head. As you hit the ball, throw your weight into your stroke by leaning forward onto your left foot. Be careful not to step over the base line. Stepping over is a foot fault.

MOTHER'S OR DAD'S INITIALS AND
DATE FOR EACH CREDIT

1. _____

○ _____

○ _____

○ _____

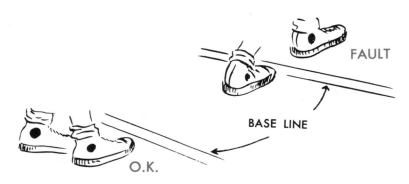

FAULT

BASE LINE

O.K.

FAULT RULES

In serving, the following count as faults:
1. Jumping so that both feet leave the ground.
2. Stepping on or over the base line before racket strikes the ball.
3. Serving into wrong court or from wrong side of center mark.
4. Missing the ball completely.
5. Causing the ball to hit something, other than the net, before it touches the ground.

When you make one of these faults, you may try to serve correctly only once more for the same point.

BASEBALL

PITCHER— Your job is to throw the ball to the batter so he strikes out or hits the ball to one of the fielders who can put him out. Learning to pitch with enough speed and control to fool the batter calls for lots of practice. Aim for the corners of the plate, high or low—wherever the batter finds it hardest to hit. A pitcher must also field bunts. He covers first base when the ball is hit to the first baseman.

INFIELDER— Playing first, second or third base or shortstop, you handle a lot of "grounders" and pop flies from the batter. You throw and catch throws from other fielders. You "cover" your base—try to put out any runner as he tries to reach your base.

OUTFIELDER— In the outfield you learn to decide quickly where long flies are going to come down. You run fast enough to catch them for the out. You must have a long throw to get the ball back to an infielder. Never hold onto the ball when there are men on bases. Often you throw the ball to the base ahead of the runner nearest home.

ROWING

Hold oar handles firmly, knuckles up, wrists and arms straight, body bent forward. Drop oar blades, edges first, into water—not too deep.

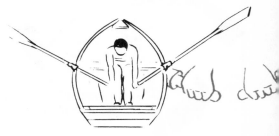

Lean back slowly, bend your arms and pull hard on blades against the water until your elbows come in against your ribs.

Lift oar blades a little out of the water and turn your knuckles up toward your face. This turns the blades flat to the water's surface.

Return to the first position, bending forward, straightening your wrists and arms. To row backward, push on the oars instead of pulling.

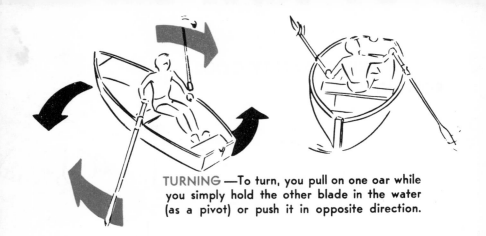

TURNING —To turn, you pull on one oar while you simply hold the other blade in the water (as a pivot) or push it in opposite direction.

ARCHERY

To shoot, stand with your left side toward target. Lay an arrow across the bow. Fit it to the bowstring. Nock it with colored cock feather standing up, between your first and second fingers. Raise your left arm with a very slight bend at the elbow. Pull the drawstring back slowly with your first, second and third fingers. The arrow rests on your left hand against the left side of the bow. The tip of your right forefinger comes back to your chin. Your elbow is as high as your shoulder. Aim, then relax your three drawing fingers so that the bowstring and arrow slip smoothly out.

SAFETY RULES

1. Never nock an arrow until you are ready to shoot.
2. Never aim an arrow in the direction of anyone.
3. Shoot only where you have a clear view all around you.

THE SKIER'S SAFETY CODE

1. Ski only when properly equipped and properly clothed.
2. Never ski alone.
3. Ski under control, which means being able to turn and stop at will.
4. Ski only on slopes suited to ability.
5. Try to check trail before skiing down it.

GETTING UP

KICK TURN

PROPER SKI EQUIPMENT

Ski boots should be roomy enough for one pair of cotton socks and one pair of woolen socks. Ski bindings must be capable of holding the boot firmly to the ski, with no give or side play when adjusted. Ski clothing should consist of wool underwear and socks, ski pants, wool shirt or sweater, windbreaker jacket, winter cap with earlaps, mittens, and dark glasses. Ski poles should be high enough to reach almost to the armpits. Skis made of hickory are the most popular, but ash, birch, or maple skis are good. The length of the skis should be your height plus 10 inches. Steel edges are very helpful where heavy ski traffic creates hard-packed snow.

SAFETY RULES FOR ICE SKATING

1. Always use sharp skates.
2. Skate only on approved ice surfaces.
3. Never skate alone.
4. Watch where you are skating at all times.
5. Never throw anything on the ice.
6. Never push or grab another skater.

MORE THINGS TO DO

(Ask dad or mother to help read the hard words.)

SAWING AND HAMMERING

CROSS CUT SAW

First draw a straight line to follow. Then hold your board firmly on a bench or on sawhorses. Start gently, then use fairly long strokes. Don't press—let the saw do its work. Use your left hand as a guide, but keep your thumb raised away from the teeth. Look straight down and follow the line.

Hold nail between your thumb and fore-finger, and tap it a few times to get it started. Then you can take your hand away and drive harder. "Toe" nailing mean driving a nail on a slant so it will hold wel Below you see how to clinch a nail.

TOE NAILING AND CLINCHING

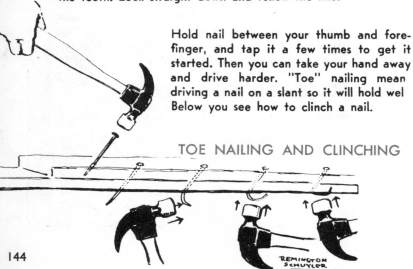

PAINT

The day before you plan to use a can of paint, turn it upside down so that lead, oil and turpentine will mix. Very little stirring is then necessary. Before painting a rough surface, sandpaper it. When painting, do not dip more than half of brush in paint. Use regular strokes, following grain of the wood. Slant the brush slightly so that the bristles will trail smoothly with each stroke. To leave a brush unwashed overnight, hang it on a wire or loop of string so that bristles are in water (as in cross-section of can shown at bottom).

SANDPAPER

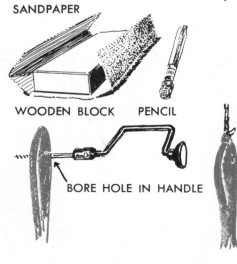

WOODEN BLOCK   PENCIL

BORE HOLE IN HANDLE

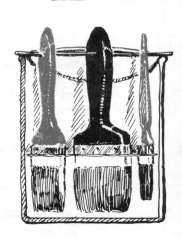

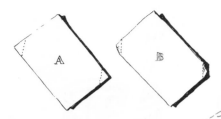

TRICKS
AND PUZZLES

FLOP THE CARD

Bend opposite corners of a postcard downward (A and B above), and place it on a table, standing on the points (C). Ask someone to turn it upside down without touching it. *How to do it:* Clap your hands together. This should make enough wind to flop the card over (D).

DROP THE COIN

Place a card on top of a glass of water and put a coin in the center of it, as shown at right below. Ask someone if he can drop the coin into the glass without touching it. *How to do it:* Hit one corner of the card sharply with a pencil.

MAGIC PADDLE

A popsickle stick will do for the paddle. Put peg through hole about center. Mark two dots below peg on one side, one on each side of peg on other. Show audience one side of paddle. Then swing it overhead, flipping paddle over so that you now show other side with dots moved.

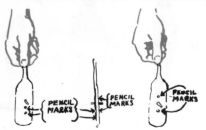

PENCIL MARKS

PENCIL MARKS

PENCIL MARKS

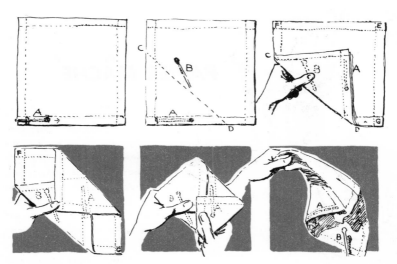

MATCH TRICK

Put match A through hole in hem of handkerchief (do this secretly). Then let audience see you place match B on handkerchief as shown. Fold corner over match B along line C-D. Holding match B with your thumb and forefinger, fold over corners E, F, and G. Then let someone break match A (the one in the hem) and shake unbroken match B out.

COIN TRICK

Lay out three pennies so distance from A to B is same as C-D. Ask audience to guess which distance is greater. Answer—both are the same.

SAUSAGE FINGER

Place tips of your forefingers together three inches before your eyes. You will see a small "sausage" appear between them. Pull your fingers apart and watch sausage disappear.

PAPIER MÂCHÉ

Papier-mâché (say *paper ma-shay'*) is French for "chewed paper." And that is just what you use to make it. Tear newspapers into bits about an inch square, and mix with hot water, flour and glue sizing. Knead this mixture into a smooth paste, as shown at left, until it is free of lumps. Then you will have a thick material which you can mold into any shape you wish, and allow it to harden. Why don't you mold a bowl by shaping some papier-mâché inside another bowl. Or make animal statuettes or an adobe house like the one which is shown below.

YOU CAN MAKE AN ADOBE HOUSE

LEATHER CRAFT

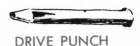

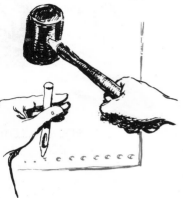

MARKING WHEEL

BROOM HANDLE

NAIL →

← WIRE

CLOTHES PIN

ALARM CLOCK WHEEL

You can make a very satisfactory marking wheel and hole-punch out of scrap materials. To make the wallet shown below, mark and punch holes, then lace with thong.

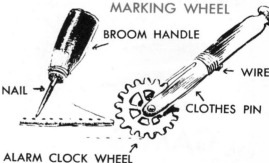

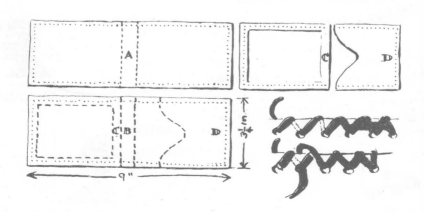

A

C D

C B D

3½"

5

9"

SHUTTLECOCK

Stick points of three feathers into pieces of cardboard, bend quills over, tape down, pad with cotton and cover with toe of sock as shown. Rig up net between two trees or poles. Game is played like deck tennis, tossing shuttlecock back and forth.

ROUND CLOTH

FEATHER

STRING

GAMES

SHADOW PICTURES

Use at least a 125-watt lamp, and shut out all other light in the room. A Cub Scout stands where the light will throw a shadow of his face and shoulders onto a sheet of paper tacked on the wall. Draw the outline on the paper and fill in with black crayon. See who can make the best silhouette.

SILHOUETTE

LIGHT

ARTIST

PROFILE

DRAW OUTLINE

GO TO IT

REMINGTON SCHUYLER

POLE

1. Cut rockers A and B out of 1-inch board. 2. Notch and fit them together. 3. Screw circular top of board to rockers.

SIDEWALK SHUFFLE BOARD

Mark off the diagram below on a sidewalk. Make pushers and wooden disks. From a starting line, first one player, then the other, pushes a disk until each has pushed six. Object is to put your disks in highest numbered spaces and to knock your opponent's out. Disks that touch a line do not count.

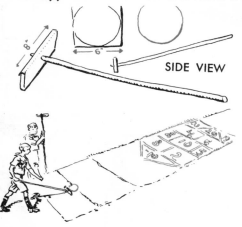

SIDE VIEW

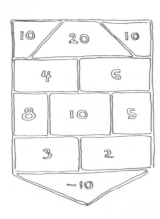

START SCREW WITH HAMMER

CENTER PUNCH FROM NAIL AND SPOOL

SCREW DRIVER

First make a center punch from a spool and nail, as shown above. This is used to start holes for screws. Start a screw straight in with a tap of a hammer. Then finish with the screw driver. The diagrams at left and bottom left show how to use either flat-head or round-head screws in making a folding-top desk to set on a stand or table.

AWL

FRONT

DRAWER

REMINGTON SCHUYLER

ANVIL

Here is how you can make your own awl out of scrap. Soap the point of a large finishing nail and carefully drive it a half-inch through a section of broom handle (see right). Bend the nail point down around the handle. Flatten the head on an iron bar or stone and file it until the proper drill point is made.

YOUR DEN

What Is a Den?

Your Den is a group of boys in your neighborhood with whom you play almost every day. You will have a meeting one afternoon a week and have a lot of fun.

Your Den Chief

A Boy Scout will help you in your Den. He is called the Den Chief. He may have been a Cub Scout just like you when he was your age. Follow him and help him.

Your Denner

One of you is elected Denner to help the Den Chief. Some day you may be Denner.

Your Den Mother

She is a Cub Scout's mother who helps the Den Chief plan Den fun. She gives up a lot of her time to you because she likes boys.

Your Den Dad

He helps your Den Mother and Cubmaster in many ways, such as planning Dad-and-Son outings.

YOUR DEN

You will have a lot of fun at your weekly Den meetings, and you will get plenty of ideas for things to do the rest of the week. Don't miss one. Here is what happens at a Den meeting.

While Cub Scouts Gather

Always try hard to be on time at your Den meetings. You will miss some fun if you don't because while the boys are gathering for the meeting, you will have something special to do. It may be a game, some handicraft, some puzzles, or lots of other things.

Opening Ceremony

When most of the fellows have come, it's time to open the meeting. You will give your Den yell or sing your Den song, or have a flag ceremony.

Den Business

Den business is collecting dues, checking up on your Cub Scout books to see what achievements you have passed

MEETING

since the last meeting, and planning your Den's part in
Pack meetings.

Den Fun

In most of your Den meetings you will play a game, and
you will probably learn a trick or two to work on your
dad. You may start some handicraft which you can finish
at home, and you may practice your stunt for the Pack
meeting.

Closing Ceremony

After all of this is over, maybe you will join the other
Cub Scouts in the Living Circle, saying the Cub Scout
Promise. Or one of the Den leaders may tell a short story.

After the Meeting

Do everything you can to help clean up the Den meeting room. You can put things away, pick up scraps, and
try to make the Den Mother's home just as neat as it was
before the Den meeting started.

YOUR PACK

What Is a Pack?

Just as your Den is a group of your friends, a Pack is a group of Dens. Your Pack will meet one evening each month. It will be a meeting not only for you, but for your parents, too. Do everything you can to take part in every Pack meeting and get your parents to come with you.

Your Cubmaster

Your Cubmaster is a man who spends a lot of time planning and leading your Pack meeting. He meets with your Den Chiefs and Den Mothers and helps them plan your Den meetings.

Your Pack Committee

This is a group of men who help the Cubmaster. They have regular meetings and plan special Pack fun. Your Den Dad is a member of this Committee.

Your Pack Meeting

Every month your Den and Pack program will be about something different, such as Indians, a Pack Circus, Things

That Go, or Aircraft. You will have fun during the month getting ready to help put on a show at the Pack meeting.

Get to the meeting early to help set up your Den exhibits. These exhibits show everybody what you have done during the month. While the Cubmaster is meeting with your mothers and dads, you will get ready to put on your Den stunt.

The Pack Show

At each Pack meeting your Den will probably have a chance to put on a stunt. You will also see the other Dens' stunts too. It's fun watching and taking part in this big show.

Akela's Council

At each Pack meeting the Cub Scouts who have earned badges during the month will receive them in a special ceremony. Your mother and dad will be in this ceremony with you and give your badge to you.

A WORD TO PARENTS

"I wish there were some way in which I might get a little closer to my son. I try my best to understand him but the gap between his viewpoint and my more mature viewpoint is a wide one. I need a bridge to span that gap."

Have you ever said something like that? Don't be too concerned about it because almost every parent has that problem. Cub Scouting is the sort of bridge of understanding which you have been seeking.

Be patient with him; he needs your help.

You are about to enter into a great experience with your son. He will not get full value from the Cub Scouting program unless you, his parents, take an active part.

Start helping him by carefully reading "What the Achievement Plan Means to Your Son," (Page 159). Follow the suggestions and your son will get more out of his Cub Scouting experience.

If you want to know still more about the program, get the *Parents' Cub Scout Book* (No. 3821).

Work with your boy on his Bobcat requirements until he can pass them to you. Then sign his application form, showing that he has done so.

Your son's Motto as a Cub Scout is "Do Your Best." Your motto as a parent should be, "I will help my son do his best."

Best wishes as you start the Cub Scouting trail with your son.

WHAT THE ACHIEVEMENT PLAN
MEANS TO YOUR SON

1. The Cub Scout achievement plan is a device for you to use in helping your son develop physically and mentally and have fun while he is doing so.

2. The projects are things which experts have considered helpful and basic to his growth.

3. His experience with his achievements will do more than help to build his self-reliance. It will also help him toward the discovery that he is now old enough to meet certain responsibilities toward other people. This is necessary as a foundation to good citizenship.

4. The plan also provides a means of giving your boy the recognition he needs so much. Boys often develop behavior problems in seeking recognition. If he receives proper recognition he may not have to do so many exasperating things in seeking it.

WHAT THE ACHIEVEMENT PLAN MEANS
TO YOUR FAMILY

1. The achievement plan can help to provide the basis for a rich family life. Many of the projects are such that the entire family can enjoy them together.

YOUR PART IN MAKING THE PLAN WORK

1. Since Cub Scouting is a program for families and not merely a program for boys, it is only natural that the achievement plan is given a family emphasis.

2. The thing which most determines what your boy will get from his Cub Scouting experience is the amount of interest and cooperation which he receives from you.

3. Not only will your boy pass his achievements to you, but he will also need help and encouragement from you in his preparation for passing them. Your eight-year-old will not be able to accomplish some of his achievement projects without your help.

4. Through working with him, you will learn to know him. You will be influencing his attitudes toward you and his home. That is important enough to be worth the sacrifice you must make.

5. You are expected—to work with your son on preparing his achievements.

   You are expected—to give your son the opportunity of passing his achievements to you. Who, better than yourself, knows when he is doing his best?

   You are expected—to participate in all achievement ceremonies when your boy receives his badges. Indeed, you will be asked to present his badges to him.

HOW THE ACHIEVEMENT PLAN WORKS

If your son enters at the age of eight:

1. First your boy must complete his Bobcat requirements. They are explained on pages 4-10 of his Wolf book. You'll probably find that he will need your help in two ways.

2. First, he may find it difficult to read the material—so start by having him read it aloud, helping him wherever necessary.

3. Second, he may not really understand the Cub Scout Promise and the Law of the Pack. Therefore use the material on pages 4-9 to interpret them for him.

4. When your boy is ready, he may pass his Bobcat requirements to you. Then you may sign his Cub Scout application. You will be asked to participate in the ceremony when he is given his Bobcat badge and membership certificate.

5. Now your boy is ready to begin to work on his Wolf achievements. He may do them in any order, not necessarily in the order listed. Your relationship to his progress is explained later in this book.

6. Your boy's interest in his Collection achievement can lead your family into an interesting hobby. The Scrapbook achievement can lead to the making of a handsome diary or record of your last vacation together. The Reading achievement can revive the wonderful old-fashioned custom of family reading, each member taking a turn at reading aloud from time-tested children's stories.

As a basis for passing the Helps achievement, you can have a family conference to decide what each member would like to do in the way of home jobs. This often changes a boy's attitude toward doing his part at home.

When the achievement plan is working as it should in the home, you will have the feeling that the whole family is progressing through the ranks of Cub Scouting.

THE TWELVE WOLF CUB SCOUT ACHIEVEMENTS

He'll need plenty of help from you

(A) You will find on the following pages definite tips on how to work with your boy on his Wolf achievements.

(B) They will help you to help him—and he'll need plenty of help from you if he is to get the most out of his achievements. Here are just a few general points to keep in mind:

(C) SIGNING FOR HIS ACHIEVEMENTS. As already explained, when your boy is ready to pass an achievement, he will pass it to you. If he succeeds, you will sign his *Wolf Cub Scout Book* in the place provided under that achievement.

There is no rule against both parents observing the achievement and signing for it, but only one signature is required. However, if both parents take part, the achievement becomes more of a family project and more important in your son's eyes.

When an achievement is signed, have your son take his Wolf Book to Den meeting so his Den Mother can make a record of it on the achievement wall chart.

(D) HOW MUCH CAN YOU EXPECT? This question is covered quite thoroughly under each of the achievements and under the explanation of the elective plan which you will find in this book. Keep in mind the boy's *effort* as well as his *efficiency*. How hard he *tries* is as important as how well he *does*. Improvement while he practices is often a good sign. If he needs to be encouraged, interest him in beating his own record.

More important, however, is that you know your boy well. Try to measure his efforts with a yardstick corresponding to his age. Don't apply the yardstick of adult performance.

The most significant measurement is whether he has *done his best*. With this as a standard, you will discourage him from trying to just "get by." You will help him develop the attitude expressed in the Cub Scout Motto, "Do Your Best."

(E) HOW FAST SHOULD HE ADVANCE? Ideally, he should be allowed to find his own rate of advancement. Keeping steady pace of one or two achievements a month is better than doing all twelve in one or two months. You should at least encourage him to complete the achievements required for his age.

Try to avoid over-pressure. Don't constantly remind him of the progress of other boys. Don't feel, as a matter of family pride, that he must excel or keep up with every other boy in the Den or Pack.

(F) HOW MUCH HELP SHOULD YOU GIVE? While it is true that you should have a close relationship with your boy in this experience, he also needs to feel that he is somewhat on his own. Through his years in Cub Scouting he will grow increasingly independent. You must sense this, and attempt to strike a happy medium between letting him depend upon you too much and working sufficiently closely to show you are interested and willing to help.

(G) READING THE BOOK. Most eight year old boys do not read very well. You'll find it necessary to help him in his reading. Sometimes you'll have to read aloud certain parts of the book. You'll be able to help him more effectively if you first read the *Wolf Cub Scout Book* yourself.

(H) STUDY AND TALK OVER THE PROJECTS WITH HIM. Do this ten to fifteen minutes at a time unless his interest lasts longer. Stop when he loses interest, and go back to it some other time—one of those times when he says, "What can I do now?"

FEATS OF SKILL—ACHIEVEMENT 1

This achievement was not developed merely to recognize your boy for things he can already do. Rather, **its purpose is to help him develop new physical skills.** Therefore, try to help him choose those things which will be most helpful to him, and not merely the things which he can already do. You will find him more interested in these feats if you can suggest some of the practical uses for the skills. **Help your boy to avoid becoming discouraged** if he cannot do the things at first try. He is at a stage in his development when physical coordination is not fully developed. These skills will help him develop such coordination.

1. THE ROLLS

The main purpose of the front roll, back roll, and falling roll is to develop agility in your boy. Be sure that he tucks his head under in doing the front or back roll or he may get a bump. He will be more interested in the rolls if he realizes that they will be helpful as he learns to play football. They'll teach him how to protect himself when falling.

2. PLAY CATCH

This skill will be much more fun if dad and son play catch together. Don't just invite him to pass the ball throwing skill. Instead, invite him to a game of catch. He may be quite surprised when you tell him he passed this portion of the Feats of Skill Achievement.

Be patient, dad. Being eight, your boy has by no means developed the knack of throwing straight or catching well. You can help him to like playing ball by getting him started right. Start at a shorter distance than the required twenty feet, and gradually lengthen it.

3. TREE CLIMBING

Tree climbing is a natural activity for most Cub Scout-age boys. They shinny up small trees by pulling themselves up a little at a time, using a strong footlock. Dad will remember! And caution your son about putting his full weight on branches that may be dead. Don't trust them.

4. KICK BOARD SWIM

Grasp kick board firmly. Shove off botton with feet as you

straighten out in water with legs outstretched, move feet slowly up and down, past each other. Keep practicing this kick until you get your proper rhythm. Speed it up then until you can kick evenly and rapidly. Kick your legs and paddle with your hands a little if you have to.

5. WALKING A 2" X 4"

This may seem very easy to *you,* but the eight-year-old boy does not very often find it so. Start him on a line on the floor or on the ground and suggest that he pretend he is walking a tightrope at the top of a circus tent. Then move from the line to the 2" x 4". Get your boy to practice forward, backward, and sideways. It will help if dad will set up a 2" x 4" on the ground between stakes. This is a great eye exercise and develops coordination and balance.

SPECIAL NOTE: Notice in the **Wolf Cub Scout Book** *that there is a provision for the boy whose physical condition does not permit him to do these feats. Also notice, your boy chooses only three of the feats.*

FLAG—ACHIEVEMENT 2

In preparation for your son's passing the Flag achievement, have a little chat with him. Read aloud to him the statement on page 22 of the *Wolf Cub Scout Book.* Help him to understand what the flag really means. You will be surprised how much more interested he will be in this achievement, if you prepare the way as suggested.

1. PLEDGE TO THE FLAG

Your boy probably has already learned to say the Pledge to the Flag, but it is likely that he does not really know its full meaning. Surely there are some words in the Pledge which he will not understand. Won't you take time to tell him what the Pledge really means? He will have a little difficulty pronouncing "indivisible," let alone really understanding its meaning.

Teach him to be at attention, giving the Cub Scout salute, when he gives the Pledge of Allegiance. Show him that it is not only the words but also the way in which he stands while he gives the Pledge which shows respect to the flag.

2. DEN FLAG CEREMONY

This is a project which the boy will have to do in the Den meeting. You will find three samples on page 23 of your boy's *Wolf Cub Scout Book.* He may choose one of these or you may encourage him to think up a ceremony of his own. Please explain the ceremony to him; then help him practice the ceremony in your home. When he is ready to lead the ceremony in his Den, have him call the Den Mother and ask her to arrange for it.

KEEPING WELL—ACHIEVEMENT 3

Strength means a great deal to your eight-year-old son even though he may not be greatly interested in cleanliness and health. Make sure he understands the relationship of health and cleanliness to strength. Help him to understand that what he does when he is eight and nine years old will have a great effect upon his physical well-being when he becomes old enough to play baseball and other strenuous sports. Help him to see that strength and health depend upon whether or not he follows a few simple rules in his daily life.

1. HEALTH CHECK-UP BY A DOCTOR

This is NOT required of your son for passing the Keeping Well achievement. However, the age of eight is not too soon for him to learn the importance of having a health check-up each year. Explain to him the reasons for this. It would be fine for dad to accompany his son on a visit to the doctor.

2. RULES OF CLEANLINESS

Help your boy to make a simple chart on which he can record his progress in following the rules of cleanliness. He'll be more enthusiastic about this matter if you show him that there is a "pay-off" on following these simple rules. Good health means that he will be stronger, and strength means more fun.

3. CUT ON HAND

Once there was a Cub Scout who thought he had to cut his finger in order to show what to do for a small cut on his hand. Perhaps your boy won't be so realistic in his reading of the Cub Scout achievement requirements. Just have him go through the simple motions as though he had a cut on his finger. Naturally, if he does come running to you some day with a cut finger, that is an opportunity. Prepare him in advance, however. The cut may come when he is alone and has to take care of it himself.

HELPS IN THE HOME—ACHIEVEMENT 4

As in many phases of our program which are not merely natural boy activity, your boy's attitude toward this project is of first importance. A man-to-man talk between dad and son will help to get your boy in the right frame of mind. Help him to see that certain privileges come to a boy as he grows older (getting to bed later, for example). Along with the privileges come some responsibilities toward his home and family.

1. REGULAR HOME JOBS

Ask your son to mention some of the jobs that have to be done in the home almost every day. Get him to mention some of the things that both dad and mother do. Then, lead up to the subject of what he himself might do in order to feel that he is helping at home. Guide him, but try to let him select the things that he would like to do. Then decide *with him* how long he should do these things. Next, take just a few moments and help him lay out a chart on which he can keep a record of these jobs.

2. CUB SCOUT PROMISE AND LAW OF THE PACK

Using the material on pages 4 through 7 of the *Wolf Cub Scout Book,* discuss with your boy the meaning of the Cub Scout Promise and Law of the Pack. Then, let him help you decide whether he has really done his best to live up to them. Don't expect his record to be perfect. The fact that he is trying to "Do His Best" is the important thing.

WHITTLING—ACHIEVEMENT 5

Here is a natural for dad and son. Make the most of it, dad.

1. USE AND TAKE CARE OF A JACKKNIFE

You may think that your boy of eight is too young to have a jackknife. However, even though you don't give him one, it's more than likely that one will find its way into his hands during his eighth year. The most important thing you can do is to show your boy how to use a knife safely. That's far wiser than attempting to keep a knife from him, because then if he does pick one up he'll be prepared to handle it carefully.

Dad should show his son how to open and close a knife, and how to use it safely. He must emphasize the fact that a knife is not a toy to be used in playing games, but rather a tool like a hammer and a screw driver. Show him how to sharpen it as illustrated in the *Wolf Cub Scout Book*. It is quite likely dad did some whittling when he was a boy. It's a good hobby. In teaching his son how to do it, dad will re-live a bit of his boyhood.

COLLECTIONS—ACHIEVEMENT 6

Every American boy collects things. He doesn't always use good judgment in the type of things he collects or in the way in which he takes care of his collection.

Cub Scouting attempts to teach boys to do better many of the things they prefer to do anyway. That's why we have the Collections achievement—in order that we might channel a perfectly natural boy urge in the direction in which it will give him the greatest possible satisfaction. Therefore, dad should show his son how much fun it is to collect some definite item and mount his collection in such a way that he will be proud to have it in his room or to show it to his friends. Let your boy decide what he will collect. One further tip—once he decides what he is going to collect don't shower so many of the items upon him yourself that he misses the fun of picking up his own. You might suggest where or how he can find things. You and your boy can decide how many items he should have in his collection, which will be determined largely by the type of collection he makes.

SCRAPBOOK—ACHIEVEMENT 7

Here's one that requires careful approach by dad and mother. Frankly, it isn't much fun just to make a scrapbook for the sake of making a scrapbook. In fact, this achievement is not included merely to get your son to make a scrapbook, but rather to encourage him to develop a new interest or hobby.

There are two types of scrapbooks. One is the illustrated diary type, in which your boy writes the story of a vacation trip, a year in the life of his Den, or an experience in his neighborhood. He illustrates this story with rough sketches of his own, snapshots, or material from magazines or newspapers.

The other type of scrapbook is one that deals with a subject in which he has real interest. For example, he might be interested in railroading, airplanes, baseball, farming, etc. He collects all of the information and pictures he can on this subject and makes it into a scrapbook.

Help your boy decide which type of scrapbook he would like to make.

TYING THINGS—ACHIEVEMENT 8

At eight, your son is dependent upon you for many things. He doesn't like to feel dependent, however, and grasps for things that he can do for himself—especially things that may make him feel more grown up. This achievement will help give him that feeling.

1. WRAPPING A PACKAGE

There are many adults who still find it very difficult to wrap a package. The ability to do this neatly and securely comes only with practice. If you work with your boy on this, you may even improve your own gift wrapping ability.

2. TYING SHOELACES

You will notice on page 38 in the *Wolf Cub Scout Book* that your boy is asked to tie his shoelaces with a square bow knot. That's the type of knot which does not come untied, and it's the best possible way to eliminate the average boy's habit of having his shoelaces dragging behind him.

Of course, you won't expect him to figure out how to tie the square bow knot from the diagrams. They are placed in the book to help you. He will learn much more quickly if you teach him to tie the knot.

3. TYING YOUR NECKTIE

Surely this, more than most other things, is an evidence of growing up. There seems to be no better way than the drawings on page 37 to actually show how to tie a four-in-hand knot. However, we know very well that the average eight-year-old will not be able to learn to tie his tie by following these diagrams. You will have to teach him that.

Don't face him when you teach him. Instead, stand beside him so that your left hand is on the same side his is. We'll wager you will find a look of satisfaction and pride on his face the first time he ties his tie without your help.

4. TIE TWO PIECES OF CORD TOGETHER WITH AN OVERHAND KNOT

Your boy will be able to tie this knot easily once he gets accustomed to simply tying two overhand knots. This one he ties by making a loop then putting the ends through and pulling them up tight. Patience, dad! Your fingers were clumsy too when you were eight years old.

SAFETY—ACHIEVEMENT 9

Most home accidents could be avoided with only a little effort. This achievement helps your boy to watch out for his own safety. This is important because you will not always be present when he meets danger.

The achievement is important also because it gets your boy thinking about the safety of others.

2. PRACTICE HOME SAFETY

It is very doubtful whether your boy realizes that hundreds of people are killed every year by falls on stairs. Very often these falls occur because of things left there. Since your boy is not the only member of your family who leaves things on stairs, you will have to be prepared for him to call to your attention things which mother and dad may leave there.

HOME GAMES—ACHIEVEMENT 10

Since Cub Scouting is a family program, it is only natural that there should be a Home Games achievement.

1. MAKE A HOMEMADE GAME AND PLAY IT WITH YOUR FAMILY OR TAKE A FAMILY WALK OR TRIP

You will find simple, homemade games illustrated on page 43. These are only samples. You can develop many more with simple household articles. For example, you can mark off a board in small squares and toss ordinary metal washers at the board.

If your boy chooses the alternative—a family walk—let him do most of the planning. He'll find it more fun if he finds himself in the position of planning an activity for the whole family. You may have to bring him down to earth a bit on this project because he may be a little over-enthusiastic regarding the distance and time involved.

KNOW YOUR NEIGHBORHOOD — ACHIEVEMENT 11

It's surprising how little a lot of us know about our own communities. It's a lot more interesting place than most of us realize. This is especially true with your boy.

He will be more interested in this achievement if he actually visits some of the important buildings which he will find suggested in the requirements.

1. IMPORTANT SPOTS IN THE COMMUNITY

Rather than merely driving past the fire station, why not actually arrange for your family to visit it and see how it operates? The same might be done with the police station, railroad station, hospital, post office, etc. However, the most important thing in this requirement is that your boy learns where these important community services are located.

2. GIVE DIRECTIONS TO FIND THE ABOVE PLACES

This is a good test of your boy's ability to express himself. He will need to find words which will guide strangers in the community to the locations listed.

READING—ACHIEVEMENT 12

In these days there are so many things for your boy to do that sometimes the wonderful world of books is neglected. Yet, much of his future enjoyment of reading will depend upon whether or not he gets the right start at the age of eight or nine. Naturally, he won't be able to read many books at the age of eight. However, he will become more interested in reading if you begin to read aloud to him. Once in a while it may be necessary for you to substitute a word for one you find in the story.

If you will surround your boy with good things to read, there will be less chance of his spending his time on less desirable things. BOYS' LIFE magazine, published by the Boy Scouts of America, is an excellent tool for dad and mother. Naturally your eight or nine-year-old boy will not be able to read all of the stories in BOYS' LIFE magazine. However, if you read them aloud to him, he will be able to understand practically all of them. You will also have the assurance that everything in that magazine has been carefully screened to make certain that it is the type of reading that will be wholesome for your boy.

1. READ TWO BOOKS

Notice that your boy is asked to get your help or the help of his teacher or librarian in selecting a list of books. He then is asked to choose two of these books. You will probably need the help of your librarian in choosing books which your eight-year-old can read without frustration. That's part of her training.

2. CARING FOR BOOKS

Here is a chance for you to teach your boy respect for books now and contribute to the development of his own library later.

THE ELECTIVE PLAN—WHAT TO DO

When your boy has completed his Wolf achievements he will receive his Wolf badge. However, he must not begin work on his Bear achievements until he becomes nine years old. While he is waiting to become nine, he may earn Arrow Points by working on the many elective projects.

The main purpose of the elective portion of the achievement plan is to encourage your boy to explore many new and interesting fields of activity. Therefore the best way for you to introduce him to this new experience is to page through with him the part of his *Wolf Cub Scout Book* which explains the electives. *Let him make his own choices of the things he would like to do.* There is a great variety of activities, and he is sure to find some things which interest him.

Please read pages 50 and 51. You will note that your son may repeat all elective subjects several times *except* those where a special limit is noted.

Since the purpose of the electives is to encourage your boy to explore many different fields, it would be unfortunate if he limited himself to many repetitions of a small number of subjects. Encourage him to try his hand in as many elective fields as possible. However, if he has special interest in any one, the way is open for him to explore it more thoroughly.

To encourage your son to do more things, it's a good idea NOT to give him credit for projects he finished before he got his Wolf badge or before he became a Cub Scout.

ARROW POINTS
SIGNING FOR THE ELECTIVES

Page 51 explains how you will fill in your boy's elective credits as he completes them. Simply write the number of the project in the circle and place the date and your initials on the line. He can also keep his box score on page 51. Each time he earns ten credits he may receive an Arrow Point.

NUMBER OF ARROW POINTS
YOUR BOY CAN EARN

For his first ten elective credits your boy will receive a Gold Arrow Point. For each additional ten credits he completes he will receive a Silver Arrow Point. While there is no limit to the number of Silver Arrow Points he may earn, you should make sure that he does them thoroughly. The average boy earns one Gold Arrow Point and one Silver while he is waiting to become old enough to start his next rank. When he becomes nine, he should immediately begin his Bear achievements.

PRIDE IN ACHIEVEMENT VS.
LEARNING TO "GET BY"

If you allow your boy to slide through his electives too easily, he will get the idea that it isn't necessary to follow the rules of the game. It is far more important that he meet the requirements carefully, than that he have Arrow Points running down the full length of his shirt tail.

Don't push him too hard. Let him advance at his own rate, but help him avoid completely bogging down and losing interest. The most effective competition, so far as the achievement plan is concerned, is self-competition. It is more wholesome for your boy to try to beat his own record than it is for him to try to keep up with or beat the record of his friends.

A DAD AND SON ADVENTURE

If you will use the elective plan as an opportunity for parent and son cooperation, you will find it a rich experience in the life of your family. Give him a hand whenever he needs it. Work with him sometimes even if he does not need help. Doing things together is the best possible way in which to build a wholesome dad and son relationship. BUT, dad, don't get so interested in the project yourself that you complete it with your son looking on!

AKELA

Many moons before the Palefaces came to America in their big ships with sky-wings, the Red men lived and hunted in the great woods and upon the broad plains of America.

Food was quite plentiful. In the water were fish and shellfish. The woods were full of game and in the trees and along the waters were many birds.

Arrows and knives, drills and tomahawks were chipped from flint. Drills and needles were shaped from bone. Skins from animals were used for clothing and for tepees. Some simple cloth was woven from grasses. Feathers and claws and teeth and shells were used as ornaments. Baskets were made from bark and twigs. Jugs and water vessels were made from clay. Canoes were made from hollowed trees or from birch bark.

In many tribes, various animals were tamed. In some, Indian maize and other plants were grown. When there was plenty of food, there was time for handicraft and painting. Picture writing began.

The Indian was deeply religious. He felt the presence of the Great Spirit at all times and in all places. Almost everything he did had some religious meaning.

Many of the tribes lived in villages of tepees or lodges. The Council of Braves was in charge and, with the Chief, debated around the Council Fire as to what should be done. Certain hunting grounds were claimed by certain tribes, and their wars were mostly about such rights.

'Twas into such a picture that the "iron-tool civilization" of the Paleface intruded. The buffalo and the deer disappeared before the railroad, the plow, the city. The hunting grounds became farms, the forests were cut out for lumber and later for paper. Before this new civilization, the Red man was pushed back—it was too strong for him. But upon this new way of life—before he was crushed by it—he left a lasting touch of character, of art, and of ideals.

In face of it all, the Indian carried himself with the dignity of self-control.

Akela and the Webelos is a fable to read with your son.

"Hoo," called the owl in the darkness, and Mowgli, the little Indian boy in the tepee below, was wide awake! While he knew the owl was no enemy, its call always made little shivers run up and down his backbone. He lay very still. His ears were wide open now.

Other sounds came out of the forest silences. One sounded like the "meow" of a great cat, and from a hill across the lake he heard a wolf call and another answer.

Once in the evening, Mowgli's father had crept with him up close to a gathering of wolves and he had watched them form a big circle about the old wolf, the leader. Mowgli almost jumped when the whole pack gave out a grand howl of welcome to the old wolf—and then the whole pack went off together to hunt, following the Old Wolf, each helping as they hunted for their food in the great woods. He thought what fun he and the other boys would have playing as wolves—and the next day they held a little Council Ring of their own. All this came quickly to mind as he heard the wolves' calls fade away.

He wasn't exactly afraid, because he had already learned that these animals were afraid of fire and outside the tepee there burned a fire, like a mute watchman on guard. Then, too, the animals had learned to be careful of humans because when one human was attacked, he had friends who came to his rescue—to help him.

But above these strange noises, Mowgli heard something different from the wild noises of the forest; it was a step. It was a step trained to be light, yet his now eager ear could catch it. It was not the step of some animal prowling about; it was a human step. He also could hear whispers, as the steps died quickly into a strained silence.

"Boom," went the deep, muffled beat of the great ceremonial drum—and then he knew that the men of the tribe were gathering for some big pow-wow. How he wished that he too could answer that call. He wanted to be a man. He wanted to do his part.

That very day he had dropped a running rabbit with his swift little arrow and had proudly brought it home to his mother. All day he had stalked and hunted and shot, had run and chased and hidden—and now—he was tired—his eyes closed.

"Hoo," said the owl in the darkness—but Mowgli's ears were shut!

THE COUNCIL FIRE CIRCLE

Meantime, things were happening at the Great Council Fire Ring on top of the cliff. Here it was they met to worship the Great Spirit. Here they met to start a hunt or warpath by asking the help of the Great Spirit. Here they met to thank Him for success. Here they met also to decide what should be done in war or peace or hunt.

Akela was the big Chief of the Webelos. Tall, stalwart, straight as an arrow, swift as an antelope, brave as a lion—he was fierce to an enemy but kind to a brother. Many trophies hung in his tepee. His father was the Son of the Sun. His totem was the Arrow of Light.

The Medicine Man and Firemaker had come early to the Council Ring, and everything was in readiness.

Firemaker had built the ceremonial fire, and as it crackled and burned tongues of flame shot upward, throwing strange shadows into the deeper darkness of the forest.

It was out of these strange silences and noises of the Great Woods that there had boomed the great tones of the stump drum as the Medicine Man beat it as a signal. Three times its heavy tone had boomed out into the night, calling the braves from the village below, lying at the edge of the lake and protected by sharp cliffs. One by one, in silence, the braves had answered and quickly scaled the narrow ledge that led to the Council Fire.

The dance began. In turn, each dancer told a story of the tribe's greatness.

One recited the old legend of the first Chief who single-handed had bested ten enemy war-canoes filled with braves. They were waiting around the point of the lake to attack the village. He swam under water and broke through each birch bark canoe in turn and then escaped. As the enemies swam ashore, his braves tomahawked and scalped them one by one.

Another told of the Chief's bear-claw necklace. One day when stalking a deer, while passing through a rocky place, the Chief found a grizzly bear about to attack an Indian boy. He dared not shoot an arrow lest he injure the boy. So rushing in, with stones he attracted the grizzly's attention and the fight began. Like boxers they dodged and rushed at each oher until the tomahawk reached its mark and brained the grizzly, saving the life of the boy. The big hide kept the Chief warm through the long cold nights. The claws became the necklace. When the boy grew up he always fought near his Chief, guarding him. And that boy was the dancer.

Another, by step and gesture, pictured the Chief chasing the buffalo. Food had been very scarce, there was hunger in the tepees, so the Chief traveled far and saw a lone buffalo, which he began to stalk. Finally, he was so close that he started to run toward the buffalo at close range. Suddenly the buffalo turned and charged straight at him. It was all so quick he could not dodge, so the Chief leaped clear over the head of the bull and quickly turning, sank his spear in the animal's shoulder. As the buffalo stumbled, the Chief found his heart with a second spear. This food brought much joy to the hungry ones.

Another told of the laws its Chief had urged for the happiness of his people. The law of the forest had been "live and let live" —*they killed nothing needlessly*. Then came Chief Akela. He taught a new law—"live and help live." His warriors were brothers. Unmatched in battle, fierce in attack, yet to their women and children they were kindness itself. With their neighbors they lived in peace, together fighting off outside invaders. Of all the tribes near the Great Woods, they gave the most care to helping their boys learn the ways of the brave.

One after another told his tale. Then all was quiet. It was silence that could be felt. Something important was about to happen!

AKELA'S LIFE STORY

Chief Akela, bright in his warrior's headdress and in ceremonial paint, stepped into the lighted circle. The tom-tom beaters began. Low and slow, then growing like a storm, they beat fiercely as the Chief told in graceful gesture of the greatness of the tribe.

His dance pictured his own life story. He told of the strength and wisdom of his father, "Arrow of Light." He told of his mother, "Kind Eyes," from whom he learned those wondrous things that mothers know. His father had helped him make a little bow and arrow, and once when an enemy would have tomahawked his mother—he, Akela, from his papoose basket, shot the pursuing enemy in the eye, and his mother escaped.

A little later he began to understand the speech and signs and calls of the Webelos.

1. Little Indian Boy.
2. Mother's name, "Kind Eyes."
3. Father's name, "Arrow of Light."
4. Was top-man of tribe (Chief).
5. Mother chased by enemy with tomahawk, little Akela shot little arrow in his eye.
6. Enemy dropped tomahawk; mother quickly took it and struck enemy twice on head, killing him.

7. They went into the woods.
8. Talked with and learned from the wolf about tracks.
9. Talked with and learned from the bear about birds.
10. Talked with the lion about "eagle-feather" (courage).

Then he was taken on little trips into the forest among the great trees and the streams. Here from the wolf he learned the language of the ground, the tracks, the ways to food. Then, from the big kindly bears he learned the secret names of trees and the calls of birds—the language of the air. But before he might become a scouting "brave" on his own, he first had to look the lion in the eye and learn the language of the stout heart—which feared nothing and which never gave up.

Then, and only then, did his father admit him to the lower ranks of the young braves.

11   12   13   14   15

11. His father had a "big heart."
12. He had the sun (or wisdom) in his head.
13. He was a great speaker.
14. He held many council fires with other tribes (treaties).
15. He stated that all men were brothers.

They had the privilege of helping the braves and thus taking a real part in the affairs of the tribe.

As he closed his dance, by gesture and sign, he told the braves that the tribe could be no greater than its boys. He said, "The future is hidden, but if we are strong and brave and help our boys to be the same, our tribe will be strong. If our boys are square and game, they will take our places and our tribe will continue to be great."

The tom-toms closed in a final burst, and all the braves gave the great guttural "How."

Then, in silence, the warriors stood beside the dying fire, with no noise save the crackle of the embers and the mysterious noises of the forest—raising the right hand toward the sky and the Great Spirit, with the left each joined in the living circle with his brothers, as a pledge to the tribe and to the Great Spirit—a pledge to the future through the present.

YOUR UNIFORM

That blue and gold Cub Scout uniform tells people you are a Cub Scout. How proud you are to wear it!

Of course the uniform alone can't make you a Cub Scout. It's sort of like wearing a swim suit. The suit does not make you a swimmer. What you DO makes you a swimmer. The suit just helps you swim better.

Your uniform helps you be a better Cub Scout. But the things you DO really make you a Cub Scout. Those things you find in the Cub Scout Promise and the Law of the Pack:

To do your best.

To do your duty to God and Country.

To be square.

To follow Akela.

To help your Pack go.

To grow with your Pack.

To give good will.

Do those seem like a lot of things to do? Every one of them is important. If you don't DO them, you are not a true Cub Scout—even if you wear the uniform. When you DO them, you are a Cub Scout—with or without a uniform.

Yes, your uniform just says to everybody, "Here is a Cub Scout!" So you try to be a real one. Then you are proud of your uniform. Everybody is proud of you, too.

EARN IT

Uniforms cost money. Your uniform means most to you when you help earn it. Maybe you can't earn money as your dad does. But you can work around home. One Cub Scout washed the dishes every night for three months to pay for his uniform. You can find ways to earn yours, too. Talk it over with dad and mother. Boy, just think of wearing a uniform you yourself have paid for!

BUY IT

Ask your Cubmaster what store sells Cub Scout uniforms. You must take to the store your membership card. That is the little card which says you belong to the Cub Scouts. Your Cubmaster signs it and gives it to you. He does that after you have done the five things to become a Bobcat (see page 3). The man at the store can sell uniforms only to Cub Scouts. Your card will show him it is OK for you to buy a uniform.

WEAR IT

Wear your uniform to Den and Pack meetings. Wear it to school and church or synagogue during Boy Scout Week in February. Wear it in Scout parades and programs.

Be sure it is clean and neat. Mother will help you on this. But you can take care of your uniform yourself. Before you put it on, brush it. After you take it off, hang it in a closet or fold it and put it away in a drawer. Take good care of your uniform, and it will look snappy.

Help mother get the badges sewed on your shirt in the right places. The pictures on the inside front and back covers and pages 2 and 188 of this book show how to wear your Cub Scout insignia. Ask your Cubmaster where to get the badges. You must show your registration card when you buy them.

Wear your neckerchief right. Page 187 tells how to do this.

MORE HELP IN BOOKS

Parents, these Cub Scout books cannot possibly deal thoroughly with all of the subjects and projects offered. For instance, even dad, unless he has some experience, will need some pretty complete diagrams and instructions to make a radio or an electric motor.

Your local public library is full of books of ideas and helps to give you more fun in Cub Scouting. Visit it today. While you are there, take a look at the following books.

Don't overlook the children's encyclopedias, such as *The Book of Knowledge, Britannica Junior, Compton's Pictured Encyclopedia,* and *The World Book Encyclopedia.* They are gold mines of help.

FAMILY FUN, GAMES, HOBBIES, PARTIES, GIFTS

Back Yard U.S.A., (Boy Scouts of America).
Codes and Secret Writing, Herbert S. Zim (Morrow).
Coinometry, R. V. Masters and Fred Reinfield (Sterling).
Cub Scout Fun Book (Boy Scouts of America).
Cub Scout Water Fun (Boy Scouts of America).
101 Funny Things to Make and Do, Paul Castle (Sterling).
Golden Book of Crafts and Hobbies, Ben Hunt (Simon and Schuster).
Here's Your Hobby, Harry Zarchy (Knopf).
Holiday Handicraft, Nina Jordan (Harcourt).
How Book of Cub Scouting (Boy Scouts of America).
Introduction to Magic, G. Sherman Ripley (Sentinel).
Junior Party Book, B. W. Carlson (Abingdon).
Photography for Boys and Girls, S. W. Bowler (Crowell).
Stamp Collecting, Roger Lewis (Knopf).

HANDICRAFT, TOOLS, RADIO, ELECTRICITY

Electrical Things Boys Like to Make, S. R. Cook (Bruce).
Fun with Science, M. Freeman and I. M. Blacker (Random House).
Let's Make a Lot of Things, Harry Zarchy (Knopf).
Let's Make More Things, Harry Zarchy (Knopf).
Let's Make Something, Harry Zarchy (Knopf).
Picture Book of Radio and Television, J. S. Meyer (Lothrop).
Sculpture, Roger Lewis (Knopf).
Woodworking, Roger Lewis (Knopf).

MODEL BOATS, AIRCRAFT, THINGS TO DO

Boats, Airplanes, Kites, A. J. LaBerge (Bennett).
Golden Book of Airplanes, Paul Jensen (Simon and Schuster).
Golden Book of Trains, Jane Werner (Simon and Schuster).
It's Easy to Fix Your Bike, J. W. McFarlane (Follett).
Model Jets and Rockets for Boys, R. F. Yates (Harper).
Model Planes for Beginners, H. H. Gilmore (Harper).
Trains, Robert Selph Henry (Bobbs-Merrill).

MAKE BELIEVE, MUSIC

Cub Scout Songbook (Boy Scouts of America).
Let's Give a Show, Bill and Sue Severn (Knopf).
Making an Orchestra, Dorothy B. Commins (Macmillan).

Picture Book of Musical Instruments, Marion Lacey (Lothrop).

Puppets & Marionettes, Roger Lewis (Knopf).

Shari Lewis Puppet Book, The, Shari Lewis (Citadel).

Special Plays for Special Days, Hark and McQueen (Plays, Inc.).

NATURE, ANIMALS, PETS, GARDENING

All About Pets, Margery Bianco (Macmillan).

All About the Weather, I. R. Tannehill (Random House).

Barnyard Family, Dorothy Hogner (Walck).

First Puppy, C. G. Osborne (Follett).

Gardening for Young People, M. G. Kains (Emerson).

Golden Book of Nature Crafts, John R. Saunders (Simon and Schuster).

Golden Nature Guides, The: Insects, Stars, Flowers, Reptiles, Trees, and Birds, Herbert S. Zim (Simon and Schuster).

How to Know the Birds, R. T. Peterson (Houghton).

Nature Crafts, Ellsworth Jagege (Macmillan).

Wonders of the Seashore, J. Berrill (Dodd).

KEEPING STRONG, SKILL, SAFETY, OUTING, SPORTS

101 Best Action Games for Boys, Lillian and Godfrey Frankel (Sterling).

Boating Is Fun, Ruth Brindze (Dodd).

First Book of Baseball, The, Benjamin Brewster (Watts).

Fun in the Water, T. K. Cureton (Association Press).
What's Inside of Me?, H. S. Zim (Morrow).

STORIES FOR FAMILY READING

Jungle Books and Just So Stories, Rudyard Kipling (Doubleday).
Legends of the United Nations, F. Frost (Whittlesey House).
Paul Bunyan Swings His Axe, D. McCormick (Caxton).
Tall Tale America, Walter Blair (Coward).
Winnie-the-Pooh, A. A. Milne (Dutton).

FOR PARENTS — ABOUT BOOKS

Bequest of Wings, Annis Duff (Viking).
Children and Books, May Arbuthnot (Scott).
First Adventures in Reading, M. L. Becker (Lippincott).
Reading with Children and Treasure for the Taking, Anne Eaton (Viking).

YOUR NECKERCHIEF

A. Roll long edge over upon itself in several flat folds to about 6" from tip of neckerchief.

B. Place around neck of V-neck shirt or over collar of official long-sleeved shirt. (The collar of a long-sleeved shirt may be turned under when wearing the neckerchief.)

C. Draw neckerchief slide over ends and adjust to fit snugly. Wear ends loose or tied in a slipknot as preferred by the pack.

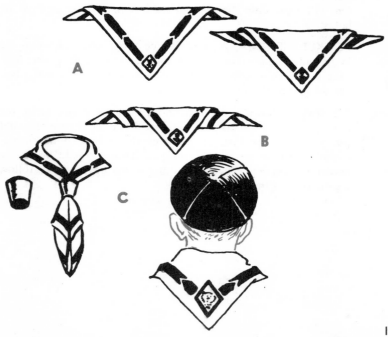

HOW TO WEAR CUB SCOUT INSIGNIA

The full-size diagrams on the inside front and back covers of this book are designed to acquaint you with the sizes, shapes, location and method, of attaching the insignia your son will be eligible to wear as a Wolf Cub Scout.

SLEEVE INSIGNIA. Use the diagram on the following page as a guide for sleeve insignia. (a) Center the edge of the page on the crease of the sleeve. (b) Line up shoulder seams of page and shirt. (c) Mark exact location of the badge with white chalk. (d) Pin to sleeve. All Cub Scouts, regardless of rank, wear the sleeve insignia indicated. Remove old insignia before attaching new. Your son will wear only the appropriate insignia of the position he holds.

POCKET INSIGNIA. As a Wolf Cub Scout, your son wears the Wolf badge centered on the left pocket, touching the pocket flap. (See inside front cover.) The gold arrow and additional silver arrows go directly below the Wolf badge.

TO SEW. Following the instructions on these pages, locate the exact position of the insignia, check with a ruler if necessary, and pin or baste to the shirt. Use a fine overhand, back, blind, or buttonhole stitch to sew on the insignia. Thread should match the border of the emblem. When using a sewing machine, follow manufacturer's instructions.